THE SPIRIT BIBLE

THE SPIRIT BIBLE

Compiled by
Eugene S. Geissler

A compilation of all the passages in Holy Scripture that mention the Spirit, together with a section on the Spirit in the Church and a concordance to the Spirit in the Bible.

Ave Maria Press
Notre Dame, Indiana 46556

Acknowledgments:

The text of The New American Bible © 1970 by the Confraternity of Christian Doctrine, Washington, D.C. (Books 1 Samuel to 2 Maccabees, 1969) is reproduced herein by license of said Confraternity of Christian Doctrine. All rights reserved.

Selections from the documents of Vatican II, *The Teachings of the Second Vatican Council,* Complete Texts of the Constitutions, Decrees and Declarations, © 1966, The Newman Press.

Nihil Obstat: John L. Reedy, C.S.C.
                  Censor Deputatus

Imprimatur: Most Rev. Leo A. Pursley, D.D.
                Bishop of Fort Wayne/South Bend

Library of Congress Catalog Card Number: 73-88004
International Standard Book Number: 0-87793-062-7

© 1973 Ave Maria Press, Notre Dame, Indiana
All rights reserved
Printed in the United States of America

Renew in our own days your miracles as of a second Pentecost . . . .

—John XXIII, 1959

We have asked ourselves on several occasions what are the greatest needs of the Church . . . . The Church needs the Holy Spirit. It needs the Holy Spirit within us, in each of us, and in all of us together, in us the Church . . . .

So let all of you ever say to him "Come!"

—Paul VI, November 1972

CONTENTS

PREFACE

This book is about the Spirit of God and the manifestation of his power.

He is the creative power hovering over the waters in the beginning. It is at beginnings that his power is most manifest and most easily recognized: at the creation of the world, at the exodus and the formation of God's people, at the founding of the kingdom; in the prophecies of a savior to come; at the incarnation, the baptism of Jesus, Pentecost, the beginning of the Church, the gospel to the Gentiles; and, looking forward, at the greatest beginning of all, Christ's second coming when "The Spirit and the Bride say, 'Come!' "

At the same time this book is about the effect of the Spirit's power on men. What a difference that power makes in individual lives: turning them around, sustaining them in a new direction, calling them to greatness: Moses, David, Isaiah, John the Baptist, Jesus himself, Peter, Paul, Stephen . . . to mention only a few . . . and what is becoming manifest in our day is that the Spirit is meant for everyone, even you and me.

Who is this Spirit? Who is this Spirit who has done all these things?

There are several ways to know the Spirit: first and best of all perhaps, is to experience him directly through his power and gifts; second, to listen to what the word of God in the bible says about the Spirit and his relationship to man; third, to hear about him from another.

This compilation from scripture is presented as a help for doing it the second way. Passages from the bible that mention the Spirit by name are collected here in the sequence of their appearance (except that in the gospel section some obvious grouping together was provided for parallel passages).

This book is not offered without apology. All of scripture is inspired of the Spirit of God and any collection such as this suffers from being only partial.

Yet, there may be some value in being introduced to the Spirit in this way, in meeting him in his own words by name, and in recognizing the abundance of his presence and the power of his action, maybe for the first time.

ESG

INTRODUCTION

In the Old Testament, the Spirit of God/Yahweh (the Lord), perceptible in the beginning as breath and wind, manifests his presence and power here and there, upon this person and that person. The Spirit of God in the Old Testament is not a person distinct from the Lord God but most often a mysterious divine energy which is clearly an important aspect of God in his dealings with man and the world. The activity of the Spirit in the Old Testament culminates in a series of prophecies concerning the One on whom the Spirit will be poured out as an anointing.

In his turn, Jesus, himself moving in the power of the Spirit, reveals to men the Father, and together they promise and send the Spirit, a third person, who comes this time as a mighty wind and fire, signaling the outpouring of the Spirit on all mankind.

In Acts, sometimes called "the Gospel of the Spirit," the Spirit completes and continues the work of Jesus Christ. By his presence in men he transforms them, and by his power he gathers together the people of God into a unity. The Acts and the Epistles are considerable evidence that the time of the fuller revelation of the Spirit is at hand.

Now, the present time is being called "the age of the Spirit."

1. The Second Vatican Council, it will be found, marked the beginning of a new time in the Church, a time inspired by the Spirit. Pope John said that the idea of the Council came to him "like a flash of heavenly light."[1] He convoked the Council with a prayer to the Holy Spirit, calling for "a new Pentecost."[2] The Council Fathers prayed to the Spirit daily.[3] In the final teachings of the Council the name and inspiration of the Holy Spirit are forcefully evident.[4]

2. Since its beginning, the liturgical renewal was taken as "a sign of God's providence in the present time, a salving action of the Holy Spirit."[5] Since the Council, the Spirit is being given renewed emphasis in the revised rites of the sacraments. In baptism men "become a new creation through water and the Holy Spirit."[6] "Signed with the gift of the Spirit in confirmation, Christians more perfectly become the image of their Lord and are filled with the Holy Spirit."[7] In the Eucharist, "They pray for a great outpouring of the Holy Spirit so that the whole human race may be brought into the unity of God's family."[8] In the revised rite of the sacrament of the sick, the formula specifically asks for "the power of his Holy Spirit"[9] in expectation of saving the sick man, as it says in James 3:13-16.[10]

3. The return to prayer at the present time also reflects the action of the Spirit among men who call God "Abba, Father" only with the help of the Spirit. "The presence of the Spirit makes prayer possible and effective."[11] The return to prayer is an almost universal movement: "The Spirit of God is calling, calling in the

12

world today, calling to communion, to covenant, to prayer . . . ."[12]

4. The Pentecostal movement in the Christian churches, and the new outpouring of the charisms of the Spirit most recently of all in the Charismatic Renewal in the Catholic Church, is a spectacular manifestation of the new age of the Spirit.[13] This manifestation is on two levels. Within each of the churches, and particularly in the Catholic Church, the Spirit is moving individuals in prayer groups to more prayer and more effective prayer, to a love of the scriptures never known before in their lives, to a greater appreciation and participation in the liturgy, and toward community in the Lord.

The other level is the ecumenical one. Without leaving their own churches, charismatic groups, if they are true to the promises and prophecies given them, are being led by the Spirit in spite of their differences toward a unity of the body of Christ seemingly impossible heretofore. This two-level manifestation is happening not in one place, or one nation, or one country, but over the whole world at the same time.

5. The call to community.[14] There has been a groundswell of new interest, and many attempts have lately been made, at "community" in various types of communes and group-together movements.[15] It is possible to discern today the movement of the Spirit toward fulfilling this very basic dimension of the radical Christian life.[16] The call to prayer is also a call to community; the same Spirit that inspires to prayer inspires those who pray together to love one another more truly and to build up the members into a close community of brothers and sisters. Prayer groups become

prayer communities, which in turn under the direction of the Spirit tend toward real communities in the Lord.[17]

6. Religious education, reflecting a convergence of these movements, is giving a new and important place to the Spirit—he through whom all things laid down by Christ are accomplished among men. "The educational mission of the Church is an integrated ministry embracing (among other things) . . . fellowship in the life of the Holy Spirit *(koinonia)*."[18] "Catechetical instruction should foster an ever-increasing awareness of the Triune God. It should enable students to grasp, through faith, the great truth that, beginning at baptism, they are called to a lifelong developing intimacy with the three divine persons."[19] "Catechetical instruction must underscore the importance and the work of the abiding Spirit of Truth in the Church and in our lives."[20]

Complementing these manifest works of the Spirit in "movements" of various kinds, there is the witness of countless individuals testifying to the activity of the Spirit in their personal lives.

NOTES

1. John XXIII, "The Opening Address of the Second Vatican Council," *The Documents of Vatican II,* copyright by the America Press, 1966, p. 712
2. See Appendix, "Prayers to the Holy Spirit," p. 238
3. *Ibid.*
4. See Appendix, "Selections from Vatican II," p. 245
5. Apostolic Constitution, Promulgation of the Roman Missal Restored . . . ," Pope Paul VI, 1969
6. "Christian Initiation, General Introduction," *The Roman Ritual,* 1969, par. 2
7. *Ibid.*
8. *Ibid.*

9. *Rites for the Sick,* International Committee on English in the Liturgy, 1971, par. 75

10. See: Apostolic Constitution on the anointing of the sick, Pope Paul VI, 1972

11. *Basic Teachings for Catholic Religious Education,* National Conference of Catholic Bishops, United States Catholic Conference, 1973, par. 14

12. Pastoral Letter, "The Lord Is Near," John Cardinal Cody, Advent 1972

13. See such books as: *The Pentecostal Movement in the Catholic Church,* Edward D. O'Connor, C.S.C., Ave Maria Press, 1971; and *Catholic Pentecostals,* Kevin and Dorothy Ranaghan, Paulist Press, 1969

14. See the emphasis on community in *To Teach as Jesus Did,* National Conference of Catholic Bishops, United States Catholic Conference, 1973, all of Part I, especially paragraphs 13, 14, 23, 24, and 28

15. See: *Communes—their goals, hopes, problems,* George R. Fitzgerald, Paulist Press, 1971

16. See: *The Church Community—Leaven & Life-Style,* Max Delespesse, Ave Maria Press, 1973

17. See: *Building Christian Communities,* Stephen B. Clark, Ave Maria Press, 1972; and *New Covenant* magazine, Catholic Charismatic Renewal Services, Ann Arbor, April 1972

18. *To Teach as Jesus Did,* National Conference of Catholic Bishops, United States Catholic Conference, 1973, par. 14

19. *Basic Teachings for Catholic Religious Education,* National Conference of Catholic Bishops, United States Catholic Conference, 1973, par. 1

20. *Op. cit.,* p. 9

PART I

THE SPIRIT IN THE OLD TESTAMENT

I. The Pentateuch

GOD'S CREATIVE AND LIFE-GIVING SPIRIT*

. . . and the Spirit of God was moving over the face of the waters

Gn 1:1

In the beginning, when God created the heavens and the earth, the earth was a formless wasteland, and darkness covered the abyss, while a mighty wind swept over the waters.

RSV reads: In the beginning God created the heavens and the earth. The earth was without form and void, and darkness was upon the face of the deep; and the Spirit of God was moving over the face of the waters.

Gn 2:7

The Lord God formed man out of the clay of the

---

*On this theme of the Spirit, see also the Wisdom books, pp. 40-45 ground and blew into his nostrils the breath of life, and so man became a living being.

Gn 6:3

Then the Lord said: "My spirit shall not remain in man forever, since he is but flesh. His days shall comprise one hundred and twenty years."

JOSEPH

. . . a man endowed with the spirit of God

Gn 41:33-41

"Therefore, let Pharaoh seek out a wise and discerning man and put him in charge of the land of Egypt. Pharaoh should also take action to appoint overseers, so as to regiment the land during the seven years of abundance. They should husband all the food of the coming good years, collecting the grain under Pharaoh's authority, to be stored in the towns for food. This food will serve as a reserve for the country against the seven years of famine that are to follow in the land of Egypt, so that the land may not perish in the famine."

This advice pleased Pharaoh and all his officials. "Could we find another like him," Pharaoh asked his officials, "a man so endowed with the spirit of God?" So Pharaoh said to Joseph: "Since God has made all this known to you, no one can be as wise and discerning as you are. You shall be in charge of my palace, and all my people shall dart at your command. Only in respect to the throne shall I outrank you. Herewith," Pharaoh told Joseph, "I place you in charge of the whole land of Egypt."

BEZALEL

. . . I have filled him with a divine spirit . . .

Ex 31:1-11

The Lord said to Moses, "See, I have chosen
Bezalel, son of Uri, son of Hur, of the tribe of Judah,
and I have filled him with a divine spirit of skill and
understanding and knowledge in every craft: in the
production of embroidery, in making things of gold,
silver or bronze, in cutting and mounting precious stones,
in carving wood, and in every other craft. As his
assistant I have appointed Oholiab, son of Ahisamach
of the tribe of Dan. I have also endowed all the experts
with the necessary skill to make all the things I have
ordered you to make: the meeting tent, the ark of the
commandments with the propitiatory on top of it, all the
furnishings of the tent, the table with its appurtenances,
the pure gold lampstand with all its appurtenances, the
altar of incense, the altar of holocausts with all its
appurtenances, the laver with its base, the service cloths,
the sacred vestments for Aaron the priest, the vestments
for his sons in their ministry, the anointing oil, and the
fragrant incense for the sanctuary. All these things they
shall make just as I have commanded you."

MOSES AND THE ELDERS

*I will take some of the spirit that is on you
and bestow it on them . . .*

Nm 11:16-17, 24-30

Then the Lord said to Moses, "Assemble for me
seventy of the elders of Israel, men you know for true
elders and authorities among the people, and bring them
to the meeting tent. When they are in place beside you,
I will come down and speak with you there. I will also
take some of the spirit that is on you and will bestow it
on them, that they may share the burden of the people
with you. You will then not have to bear it by yourself."

So Moses went out and told the people what the
Lord had said. Gathering seventy elders of the people,
he had them stand around the tent. The Lord then came
down in the cloud and spoke to him. Taking some of the
spirit that was on Moses, he bestowed it on the seventy
elders; and as the spirit came to rest on them, they
prophesied.

Now two men, one named Eldad and the other
Medad, were not in the gathering but had been left in
the camp. They too had been on the list, but had not
gone out to the tent; yet the spirit came to rest on them
also, and they prophesied in the camp. So, when a young
man quickly told Moses, "Eldad and Medad are
prophesying in the camp," Joshua, son of Nun, who from
his youth had been Moses' aide, said, "Moses, my lord,
stop them." But Moses answered him, "Are you jealous
for my sake? Would that all the people of the Lord
were prophets! Would that the Lord might bestow his
spirit on them all!" Then Moses returned to the camp,
along with the elders of Israel.

BALAAM

The spirit of God came upon him, and he gave
  voice to this oracle . . .

Nm 24:1-13

Balaam, however, perceiving that the Lord was pleased to
bless Israel, did not go aside as before to seek omens,
but turned his gaze toward the desert. When he raised
his eyes and saw Israel encamped, tribe by tribe, the
spirit of God came upon him, and he gave voice to his
oracle:

> The utterance of Balaam, son of Beor,
>   the utterance of the man whose eye is true,
> The utterance of one who hears what God says,
>   and knows what the Most High knows,
> Of one who sees what the Almighty sees,
>   enraptured, and with eyes unveiled:
> How goodly are your tents, O Jacob;
>   your encampments, O Israel!
> They are like gardens beside a stream,
>   like the cedars planted by the Lord.
> His wells shall yield free-flowing waters,
>   he shall have the sea within reach;
> His king shall rise higher than . . . .
>   and his royalty shall be exalted.
> It is God who brought him out of Egypt,
>   a wild bull of towering might.
> He shall devour the nations like grass,
>   their bones he shall strip bare.
> He lies crouching like a lion,
>   or like a lioness; who shall arouse him?

Blessed is he who blesses you,
and cursed is he who curses you!

Balak beat his palms together in a blaze of anger at
Balaam and said to him, "It was to curse my foes that
I summoned you here; yet three times now you have even
blessed them instead! Be off at once, then, to your home.
I promised to reward you richly, but the Lord has
withheld the reward from you!" Balaam replied to
Balak, "Did I not warn the very messengers whom you
sent to me, 'Even if Balak gave me his house full of
silver and gold, I could not of my own accord do
anything, good or evil, contrary to the command of the
Lord'? Whatever the Lord says I must repeat."

JOSHUA

Now, Joshua, was filled with the spirit of wisdom . . .

Nm 27:15-23

Then Moses said to the Lord, "May the Lord, the God
of the spirits of all mankind, set over the community a
man who shall act as their leader in all things, to guide
them in all their actions; that the Lord's community
may not be like sheep without a shepherd." And the
Lord replied to Moses, "Take Joshua, son of Nun, a man
of spirit,* and lay your hand upon him. Have him
stand in the presence of the priest Eleazar and of the
whole community, and commission him before their
eyes. Invest him with some of your own dignity, that
the whole Israelite community may obey him. He shall
present himself to the Priest Eleazar, to have him seek
out for him the decisions of the Urim in the Lord's

---

*RSV reads: . . . a man in whom is the spirit. . . .

presence; and as he directs, Joshua, all the Israelites with him, and the community as a whole shall perform all their actions."

Moses did as the Lord had commanded him. Taking Joshua and having him stand in the presence of the priest Eleazar and of the whole community, he laid his hands on him and gave him his commission, as the Lord had directed through Moses.

Dt 34:9-12

Now Joshua, son of Nun, was filled with the spirit of wisdom, since Moses had laid his hands upon him; and so the Israelites gave him their obedience, thus carrying out the Lord's command to Moses.

Since then no prophet has arisen in Israel like Moses, whom the Lord knew face to face. He had no equal in all the signs and wonders the Lord sent him to perform in the land of Egypt against Pharaoh and all his servants and against all his land, and for the might and the terrifying power that Moses exhibited in the sight of all Israel.

2. The Historical Books

THE JUDGES

The spirit of the Lord came upon . . . the Judges

OTHNIEL

Jgs 3:10-11

But when the Israelites cried out to the Lord, he raised up for them a savior, Othniel, son of Caleb's younger brother Kenaz, who rescued them. The spirit of the Lord came upon him, and he judged Israel. When he went out to war, the Lord delivered Cushanrishathaim, king of Aram, into his power, so that he made him subject. The land then was at rest for forty years, until Othniel, son of Kenaz, died.

GIDEON

Jgs 6:34-41; 7:9

The spirit of the Lord enveloped Gideon; he blew the horn that summoned Abiezer to follow him. He sent messengers, too, throughout Manasseh, which also obeyed his summons; through Asher, Zebulun and Naphtali, likewise, he sent messengers and these tribes advanced to meet the others. Gideon said to God, "If indeed you are going to save Israel through me, as you promised, I am putting this woolen fleece on the threshing floor. If dew comes on the fleece alone, while the ground is dry, I shall know that you will save Israel through me, as you promised." That is what took place. Early the next morning he wrung the dew from the fleece, squeezing out of it a bowlful of water. Gideon then said to God, "Do not be angry with me if I speak once more. Let me make just one more test with the fleece. Let the fleece alone be dry, but let there be dew on all the ground." That night God did so; the fleece alone was dry, but there was dew on all the ground. . . .

That night the Lord said to Gideon, "Go, descend on the camp, for I have delivered it up to you."

JEPHTHAH

Jgs 11:4-12; 27-29; 32-33; 12:7

Some time later, the Ammonites warred on Israel. When this occurred the elders of Gilead went to bring Jephthah from the land of Tob. "Come," they said to Jephthah, "be our commander that we may be able to fight the Ammonites." "Are you not the ones who hated me and drove me from my father's house?" Jephthah replied to the elders of Gilead. "Why do you come to me now, when you are in distress?" The elders of Gilead said to Jephthah, "In any case, we have now come back to you; if you go with us to fight against the Ammonites, you shall be the leader of all of us who dwell in Gilead." Jephthah answered the elders of Gilead, "If you bring me back to fight against the Ammonites and the Lord delivers them up to me, I shall be your leader." The elders of Gilead said to Jephthah, "The Lord is witness between us that we will do as you say."

So Jephthah went with the elders of Gilead, and the people made him their leader and commander. In Mizpah, Jephthah settled all his affairs before the Lord. Then he sent messengers to the king of the Ammonites to say, "What have you against me that you come to fight with me in my land? . . . I have not sinned against you, but you wrong me by warring against me. Let the Lord, who is judge, decide this day between the Israelites and the Ammonites!" But the king of the Ammonites paid no heed to the message Jephthah sent him.

The spirit of the Lord came upon Jephthah. He passed through Gilead and Manasseh, and through Mizpah-Gilead as well, and from there he went on to the Ammonites . . . to fight against them, and the Lord delivered them into his power, so that he inflicted a severe defeat on them, from Aroer to the approach of Minnith (twenty cities in all) and as far as Abelkeramin. Thus were the Ammonites brought into subjection by the Israelites. . . .

After having judged Israel for six years, Jephthah the Gileadite died and was buried in his city of Gilead.

SAMSON

Jgs 13:24-25; 14:5-6; 15:13-16, 20

The woman (wife of Manoah) bore a son and named him Samson. The boy grew up and the Lord blessed him; the spirit of the Lord first stirred him in Mahaneh-dan, which is between Zorah and Eshtaol. . . .

So Samson went down to Timnah with his father and mother. When they had come to the vineyards of

Timnah, a young lion came roaring to meet him. But the spirit of the Lord came upon Samson, and although he had no weapons, he tore the lion in pieces as one tears a kid. . . .

So they bound him with two new ropes and brought him up from the cliff. When he reached Lehi, and the Philistines came shouting to meet him, the spirit of the Lord came upon him: the ropes around his arms became as flax that is consumed by fire and his bonds melted away from his hands. Near him was the fresh jawbone of an ass; he reached out, grasped it, and with it killed a thousand men. Then Samson said,

> With the jawbone of an ass
>   I have piled them in a heap;
> With the jawbone of an ass
>   I have slain a thousand men."

Samson judged Israel for twenty years in the days of the Philistines.

SAUL

. . . and the spirit of God rushed upon him . . .

1 Sm 10:1-13

Then, from a flask he had with him, Samuel poured oil on Saul's head; he also kissed him, saying: "The Lord anoints you commander over his heritage. You are to govern the Lord's people Israel, and to save them from the grasp of their enemies round about.

"This will be the sign for you that the Lord has anointed you commander over his heritage: When you leave me today, you will meet two men near Rachel's tomb at Zelzah in the territory of Benjamin, who will say to you, 'The asses you went to look for have been found. Your father is no longer worried about the asses, but is anxious about you and says, What shall I do about my son?' Farther on, when you arrive at the terebinth of Tabor, you will be met by three men going up to God at Bethel; one will be bringing three kids, another three loaves of bread, and the third a skin of wine. They will greet you and offer you two wave offerings of bread, which you will take from them. After that you will come to Gibeath-elohim, where there is a garrison of the Philistines. As you enter that city, you will meet a band of prophets, in a prophetic state, coming down from the high place preceded by lyres, tambourines, flutes and harps. The spirit of the Lord will rush upon you, and you will join them in their prophetic state and will be changed into another man. When you see these signs fulfilled, do whatever you judge feasible, because God is with you. Now go down ahead of me to Gilgal, for I shall come down to you, to offer holocausts and to sacrifice peace offerings. Wait seven days until I come to you; I shall then tell you what you must do."

As Saul turned to leave Samuel, God gave him another heart. That very day all these signs came to pass. . . . When they were going from there to Gibeath, a band of prophets met him, and the spirit of God rushed upon him, so that he joined them in their prophetic state.

When all who had known him previously saw him in a prophetic state among the prophets, they said to one another, "What has happened to the son of Kish? Is Saul also among the prophets?" And someone from that district added, "And who is their father?" Thus the proverb arose, "Is Saul also among the prophets?" When he came out of the prophetic state, he went home.

DAVID

. . . the spirit of the Lord rushed upon David

1 Sm 16:1-13

The Lord said to Samuel: "How long will you grieve for
Saul, whom I have rejected as king of Israel? Fill your
horn with oil, and be on your way. I am sending you to
Jesse of Bethlehem, for I have chosen my king from
among his sons." But Samuel replied: "How can I go?
Saul will hear of it and kill me." To this the Lord
answered: "Take a heifer along and say, 'I have come to
sacrifice to the Lord.' Invite Jesse to the sacrifice, and
I myself will tell you what to do; you are to anoint for
me the one I point out to you."

Samuel did as the Lord had commanded him. When
he entered Bethlehem, the elders of the city came
trembling to meet him and inquired, "Is your visit
peaceful, O seer?" He replied: "Yes! I have come to
sacrifice to the Lord. So cleanse yourselves and join me
today for the banquet." He also had Jesse and his sons
cleanse themselves and invited them to the sacrifice. As
they came, he looked at Eliab and thought, "Surely the
Lord's anointed is here before him." But the Lord said to
Samuel: "Do not judge from his appearance or from his
lofty stature, because I have rejected him. Not as man
sees does God see, because man sees the appearance but
the Lord looks into the heart." Then Jesse called
Abinadab and presented him before Samuel, who said,
"The Lord has not chosen him." Next Jesse presented
Shammah, but Samuel said, "The Lord has not chosen
this one either." In the same way Jesse presented seven
sons before Samuel, but Samuel said to Jesse, "The Lord
has not chosen any one of these." Then Samuel asked

31

Jesse, "Are these all the sons you have?" Jesse replied, "There is still the youngest, who is tending the sheep." Samuel said to Jesse, "Send for him; we will not begin the sacrificial banquet until he arrives here." Jesse sent and had the young man brought to them. He was ruddy, a youth handsome to behold and making a splendid appearance. The Lord said, "There—anoint him, for this is he!" Then Samuel, with the horn of oil in hand, anointed him in the midst of his brothers; and from that day on, the spirit of the Lord rushed upon David. When Samuel took his leave, he went to Ramah.

SAUL AND DAVID

The spirit of the Lord had departed from Saul . . .

1 Sm 16:14-23

The spirit of the Lord had departed from Saul, and he was tormented by an evil spirit sent by the Lord. So the servants of Saul said to him: "Please! An evil spirit from God is tormenting you. If your lordship will order it, we, your servants here in attendance on you, will look for a man skilled in playing the harp. When the evil spirit from God comes over you, he will play and you will feel better." Saul then told his servants, "Find me a skillful harpist and bring him to me." A servant spoke up to say: "I have observed that one of the sons of Jesse of Bethlehem is a skillful harpist. He is also a stalwart soldier, besides being an able speaker, and handsome. Moreover, the Lord is with him."

Accordingly, Saul dispatched messengers to ask Jesse to send him his son David, who was with the flock. Then Jesse took five loaves of bread, a skin of wine, and a kid, and sent them to Saul by his son David. Thus

David came to Saul and entered his service. Saul became
very fond of him, made him his armor-bearer, and sent
Jesse the message, "Allow David to remain in my service,
for he meets with my approval." Whenever the spirit
from God seized Saul, David would take the harp and
play, and Saul would be relieved and feel better, for the
evil spirit would leave him.

. . . an evil spirit from God came over Saul . . .

1 Sm 18:6-16

At the approach of Saul and David (on David's return
after slaying the Philistine), women came out from each
of the cities of Israel to meet King Saul, singing and
dancing, with tambourines, joyful songs, and sistrums.
The women played and sang:

> "Saul has slain his thousands,
> and David his ten thousands."

Saul was very angry and resentful of the song, for he
thought: "They give David ten thousands, but only
thousands to me. All that remains for him is the
kingship." [And from that day on, Saul was jealous of
David.]
[The next day an evil spirit from God came over
Saul, and he raged in his house. David was in attendance,
playing the harp as at other times, while Saul was
holding his spear. Saul poised the spear, thinking to nail
David to the wall, but twice David escaped him] Saul
then began to fear David, [because the Lord was with
him, but had departed from Saul himself.] Accordingly,

Saul removed him from his presence by appointing him a field officer. So David led the people on their military expeditions, and prospered in all his enterprises, for the Lord was with him. Seeing how successful he was, Saul conceived a fear of David; on the other hand, all Israel and Judah loved him, since he led them on their expeditions.

. . . the spirit of God came upon him also . . .

1 Sm 19:8-10, 18-24

When war broke out again, David went out to fight against the Philistines and inflicted a great defeat upon them, putting them to flight. Then an evil spirit from the Lord came upon Saul as he was sitting in his house with spear in hand and David was playing the harp nearby. Saul tried to nail David to the wall with the spear, but David eluded Saul, so that the spear struck only the wall, and David got away safe. . . .

Thus David got safely away; he went to Samuel in Ramah, informing him of all that Saul had done to him. Then he and Samuel went to stay in the sheds. When Saul was told that David was in the sheds near Ramah, he sent messengers to arrest David. But when they saw the band of prophets, presided over by Samuel, in a prophetic frenzy, they too fell into the prophetic state. Informed of this, Saul sent other messengers, who also fell into the prophetic state. For the third time Saul sent messengers, but they too fell into the prophetic state.

Saul then went to Ramah himself. Arriving at the cistern of the threshing floor on the bare hilltop, he inquired, "Where are Samuel and David?" and was told, "At the sheds near Ramah." As he set out from the hilltop toward the sheds, the spirit of God came upon him also, and he continued on in a prophetic condition until he reached the spot. At the sheds near Ramah he, too, stripped himself of his garments and he, too, remained in the prophetic state in the presence of Samuel; all that day and night he lay naked. That is why they say, "Is Saul also among the prophets?"

AMASAI

Then the spirit enveloped Amasai, the chief of the Thirty . . .

1 Ch 12:17-19

Some Benjamites and Judahites also came to David at the stronghold. David went out to meet them and addressed them in these words: "If you come peacefully, to help me, I am of a mind to have you join me. But if you have come to betray me to my enemies though my hands have done no wrong, may the God of our fathers see and punish you."

Then the spirit enveloped Amasai, the chief of the Thirty, who spoke:

"We are yours, O David,
    we are with you, O son of Jesse.
Peace, peace to you,
    and peace to him who helps you;
    your God it is who helps you."

So David received them and placed them among the leaders of his troops.

DAVID'S LAST WORDS

The spirit of the Lord spoke through me . . .

2 Sm 23:1-2

These are the last words of David:

> "The utterance of David, son of Jesse;
>   the utterance of the man God raised up,
> Anointed by the God of Jacob,
>   favorite of the Mighty One of Israel.
> The spirit of the Lord spoke through me;
>   his word was on my tongue."

ELISHA SUCCEEDS ELIJAH

May I receive a double portion of your spirit?

2 Kgs 2:9-18

When they had crossed over, Elijah said to Elisha, "Ask for whatever I may do for you, before I am taken from you." Elisha answered, "May I receive a double portion of your spirit." "You have asked something that is not easy," he replied. "Still, if you see me taken up from you, your wish will be granted; otherwise not." As they walked on conversing, a flaming chariot and flaming horses came between them, and Elijah went up to heaven in a whirlwind. When Elisha saw it happen he cried out, "My father! my father! Israel's chariots and drivers!" But when he could no longer see him, Elisha gripped his own garment and tore it in two.

Then he picked up Elijah's mantle which had fallen from him, and went back and stood at the bank of the Jordan. Wielding the mantle which had fallen from Elijah, he struck the water in his turn and said, "Where is the Lord, the God of Elijah?" When Elisha struck the water it divided and he crossed over.

The guild prophets in Jericho, who were on the other side, saw him and said, "The spirit of Elijah rests on Elisha." They went to meet him, bowing to the ground before him. "Among your servants are fifty brave men," they said. "Let them go in search of your master. Perhaps the spirit of the Lord has carried him away to some mountain or some valley." "Do not send them," he answered. However, they kept urging him, until he was embarrassed and said, "Send them." So they sent the fifty men, who searched for three days without finding him. When they returned to Elisha in Jericho, where he was staying, he said to them, "Did I not tell you not to go?"

CYRUS INSPIRED

The Lord inspired King Cyrus of Persia

Ezr 1:1-5

In the first year of Cyrus, king of Persia, in order to fulfill the word of the Lord spoken by Jeremiah, the Lord inspired King Cyrus of Persia to issue this proclamation throughout his kingdom both by word of mouth and in writing:

"Thus says Cyrus, king of Persia: 'All the kingdoms of the earth the Lord, the God of heaven, has given to me,

37

and he has also charged me to build him a house in Jerusalem, which is in Judah. Whoever, therefore, among you belongs to any part of his people, let him go up, and may his God be with him! Let everyone who has survived, in whatever place he may have dwelt, be assisted by the people of that place with silver, gold, goods, and cattle, together with free-will offerings for the house of God in Jerusalem.' "

Then the family heads of Judah and Benjamin and the priests and Levites—everyone, that is, whom God had inspired to do so—prepared to go up to build the house of the Lord in Jerusalem.

THE ISRAELITES

Your good spirit you bestowed on them

Neh 9:20, 23, 30-31

Your good spirit you bestowed on them, to give them understanding; your manna you did not withhold from their mouths, and you gave them water in their thirst. . . .

You made their children as numerous as the stars of the heavens, and you brought them into the land which you had commanded their fathers to enter and possess. . . .

You were patient with them for many years, bearing witness against them through your spirit, by means of the prophets; still they would not listen. Thus you delivered them over into the power of the peoples of the lands. Yet in your great mercy you did not completely destroy them and you did not forsake them, for you are a kind and merciful God.

THE CREATING SPIRIT

You sent forth your spirit

Jdt 16:14

Let every creature serve you;
    for you spoke, and they were made,
You sent forth your spirit, and they were created;
    no one can resist your word.

3. The Wisdom Books

It is a spirit in man . . .

Jb 32:8

But it is a spirit in man,
 the breath of the Almighty,
  that gives him understanding.

For the spirit of God has made me . . .

Jb 33:3-4

I will state directly what is in my mind,
 my lips shall utter knowledge sincerely;
For the spirit of God has made me,
 the breath of the Almighty keeps me alive.

If he were to take back his spirit . . .

Jb 34:14-15

If he were to take back his spirit to himself
 withdraw to himself his breath,

All flesh would perish together,
and man would return to the dust.

THE SUSTAINING SPIRIT

. . . and your holy spirit take not from me

Ps 51:12-14

A clean heart create for me, O God,
and a steadfast spirit renew within me.
Cast me not out from your presence,
and your holy spirit take not from me.
Give me back the joy of your salvation,
and a willing spirit sustain in me.

THE RENEWING SPIRIT

When you send forth your spirit . . .

Ps 104:27-30

They all look to you
to give them food in due time.
When you give it to them, they gather it,
when you open your hand, they are filled with
good things.
If you hide your face, they are dismayed;
if you take away their breath, they perish
and return to their dust.
When you send forth your spirit, they are created,
and you renew the face of the earth.

GOD'S ALL-KNOWING SPIRIT

Where can I go from your spirit?

Ps 139:7-10

Where can I go from your spirit?
    from your presence where can I flee?
If I go up to the heavens, you are there;
    if I sink to the nether world you are present there.
If I take the wings of the dawn,
    if I settle at the farthest limits of the sea,
Even there your hand shall guide me,
    and your right hand hold me fast.

THE SPIRIT OF WISDOM

I will pour out to you my spirit . . .

Prv 1:20-23

Wisdom cries aloud in the street
    in the open squares she raises her voice;
Down the crowded ways she calls out,
    at the city gates she utters her words:
"How long, you simple ones, will you love inanity,
    how long will you turn away at my reproof?
Lo! I will pour out to you my spirit,
    I will acquaint you with my words."

THE ALL-EMBRACING SPIRIT

The spirit of the Lord fills the world . . .

Wis 1:7

For the spirit of the Lord fills the world,
    is all-embracing, and knows what man says.

. . . your holy spirit from on high

Wis 9:17

Or who ever knew your counsel,
    except you had given Wisdom
    and sent your holy spirit from on high?

Wis 12:1

For your imperishable spirit is in all things!

THE SPIRIT OF UNDERSTANDING

*Then, if it pleases the Lord Almighty, he will be filled
with the spirit of understanding . . .*

Sir 39:1-8

How different the man who devotes himself
    to the study of the law of the Most High!
He explores the wisdom of the men of old
    and occupies himself with the prophecies;
He treasures the discourses of famous men,
    and goes to the heart of involved sayings;
He studies obscure parables,

and is busied with the hidden meanings of the sages.
He is in attendance on the great,
    and has entrance to the ruler.
He travels among the peoples of foreign lands
    to learn what is good and evil among men.
His care is to seek the Lord, his Maker,
    to petition the Most High,
To open his lips in prayer,
    to ask pardon for his sins.
Then, if it pleases the Lord Almighty,
    he will be filled with the spirit of understanding;
He will pour forth his words of wisdom
    and in prayer give thanks to the Lord,
Who will direct his knowledge and his counsel,
    as he meditates upon his mysteries.
He will show the wisdom of what he has learned
    and glory in the law of the Lord's covenant.

THE FORESEEING SPIRIT

By his powerful spirit he looked into the future . . .

Sir 48:20-25

But they called upon the Most High God
    and lifted up their hands to him;
He heard the prayer they uttered,
    and saved them through Isaiah.
God struck the camp of the Assyrians
    and routed them with a plague.
For Hezekiah did what was right
    and held fast to the paths of David,
As ordered by the illustrious prophet
    Isaiah, who saw the truth in visions.
In his lifetime he turned back the sun

and prolonged the life of the king.
By his powerful spirit he looked into the future
and consoled the mourners of Zion;
He foretold what should be till the end of time,
hidden things yet to be fulfilled.

4. The Prophets

ISAIAH

THE RULE OF EMMANUEL

The spirit of the Lord shall rest upon him

Is 11:1-9

But a shoot shall sprout from the stump of Jesse,
    and from his roots a bud shall blossom.
The spirit of the Lord shall rest upon him:
    a spirit of wisdom and of understanding,
A spirit of counsel and of strength,
    a spirit of knowledge and of fear of the Lord,
    and his delight shall be the fear of the Lord.
Not by appearance shall he judge,
    nor by hearsay shall he decide,
But he shall judge the poor with justice,
    and decide aright for the land's afflicted.
He shall strike the ruthless with the rod of
       his mouth,
    and with the breath of his lips he shall slay the
        wicked.
Justice shall be the band around his waist,
    and faithfulness a belt upon his hips.

Then the wolf shall be a guest of the lamb,
    and the leopard shall lie down with the kid;
The calf and the young lion shall browse together,
    with a little child to guide them.
The cow and the bear shall be neighbors,
    together their young shall rest;
    the lion shall eat hay like the ox.
The baby shall play by the cobra's den,
    and the child lay his hand on the adder's lair.
There shall be no harm or ruin on all
        my holy mountain;
    for the earth shall be filled with knowledge
        of the Lord
    as water covers the sea.

SALVATION FROM GOD

Until the spirit from on high is poured out on us

Is 32:14-18

Yes, the castle will be forsaken,
    the noisy city deserted;
Until the spirit from on high
    is poured out on us.
Then will the desert become an orchard
    and the orchard be regarded as a forest.
Right will dwell in the desert
    and justice abide in the orchard.
Justice will bring about peace;
    right will produce calm and security.
My people will live in peaceful country,
    in secure dwellings and quiet
        resting places.

THE MAJESTY OF GOD

Who has directed the spirit of the Lord?

Is 40:12-14

Who has cupped in his hand the waters of the sea,
    and marked off the heavens with a span?
Who has held in a measure the dust of the earth,
    weighed the mountains in scales
    and the hills in a balance?
Who has directed the spirit of the Lord,
    or has instructed him as his counselor?
Whom did he consult to gain knowledge?
    Who taught him the path of judgment,
    or showed him the way of understanding?

THE SERVANT OF YAHWEH

My chosen one . . . upon whom I have put my spirit

Is 42:1-5

Here is my servant whom I uphold,
    my chosen one with whom I am pleased,
Upon whom I have put my spirit;
    he shall bring forth justice to the nations,
Not crying out, not shouting,
    not making his voice heard in the street.
A bruised reed he shall not break,
    and a smoldering wick he shall not quench,
Until he establishes justice on the earth;
    the coastlands will wait for his teaching.
Thus says God, the Lord,
    who created the heavens and stretched them out,

who spreads out the earth with its crops,
Who gives breath to its people
    and spirit to those who walk on it:

I, the Lord, have called you for the victory of justice,
    I have grasped you by the hand;
I formed you, and set you
    as a covenant of the people,
    a light for the nations,
To open the eyes of the blind,
    to bring out prisoners from confinement,
    and from the dungeon, those who live in darkness.

I am the Lord, this is my name;
    my glory I give to no other,
    nor my praise to idols.

See, the earlier things have come to pass,
    new ones I now foretell;
Before they spring into being,
    I announce them to you.

THE BLESSING OF ISRAEL

I will pour out my spirit upon your offspring . . .

Is 44:3

I will pour out water upon the thirsty ground,
    and streams upon the dry land;
I will pour out my spirit upon your offspring,
    and my blessing upon your descendants.
They shall spring up among the verdure
    like poplars beside the flowing waters.

A PROMISE

My spirit which is upon you . . . shall never leave . . .

Is 59:21

This is the covenant with them
    which I myself have made, says the Lord:
My spirit which is upon you
    and my words that I have put into your mouth
Shall never leave your mouth,
    nor the mouths of your children
Nor the mouths of your children's children
    from now on and forever, says the Lord.

THE ANOINTED ONE

The spirit of the Lord God is upon me . . .

Is 61:1-2, 6

The spirit of the Lord God is upon me,
    because the Lord has anointed me;
He has sent me to bring glad tidings to the lowly,
    to heal the brokenhearted,
To proclaim liberty to the captives
    and release to the prisoners,
To announce a year of favor from the Lord
    and a day of vindication by our God. . . .
You yourselves shall be named priests of the Lord,
    ministers of our God you shall be called.

THEY REMEMBERED THE DAYS OF OLD

Where is he who put his holy spirit in their midst?

Is 63:11-14

Then they remembered the days of old,
    and Moses, his servant;
Where is he who brought up out of the sea
    the shepherd of his flock?
Where is he who put his holy spirit
    in their midst;
Whose glorious arm
    was the guide at Moses' right;
Who divided the waters before them,
    winning for himself eternal renown;
Who led them without stumbling through the depths
    like horses in the open country,
Like cattle going down into the plain,
    the spirit of the Lord guiding them?
Thus you led your people,
    bringing glory to your name.

EZEKIEL

The spirit entered into me and set me on my feet . . .

Ez 2:1-2

When I had seen it, I fell upon my face and heard a
voice that said to me: Son of man, stand up! I wish to
speak with you. As he spoke to me, spirit entered into
me* and set me on my feet, and I heard the one who was
speaking.

---

*RSV reads: . . . the spirit entered into me . . .

Ez 3:12-15

Then spirit lifted me up, and I heard behind me the noise of a loud rumbling as the glory of the Lord rose from its place: the noise made by the wings of the living creatures striking one another, and the wheels alongside them, a loud rumbling. The spirit which had lifted me up seized me, and I went off spiritually stirred, while the hand of the Lord rested heavily upon me.

Ez 3:22-24

The hand of the Lord came upon me, and he said to me: Get up and go out into the plain, where I will speak with you. So I got up and went out into the plain, and I saw that the glory of the Lord was in that place, like the glory I had seen by the river Chebar. I fell prone, but then spirit entered into me and set me on my feet, and he spoke with me.

THE NEW COVENANT PROMISED

I will put a new spirit within them

Ez 11:5, 16-17, 19-20

Then the spirit of the Lord fell upon me, and he told me to say: Thus says the Lord; . . . Though I have removed them far among the nations and scattered them over foreign countries—and was for a while their only sanctuary in the countries to which they had gone— I will gather you from the nations and assemble you from the countries over which you have been scattered, and I will restore to you the land of Israel. . . . I will give them a new heart and put a new spirit within them;

I will remove the stony heart from their bodies, and replace it with a natural heart, so that they will live according to my statutes, and observe and carry out my ordinances; thus they shall be my people and I will be their God.

THE NEW COVENANT

I will put my spirit within you . . .

Ez 36:24-28

For I will take you away from among the nations, gather you from all the foreign lands, and bring you back to your own land. I will sprinkle clean water upon you to cleanse you from all your impurities, and from all your idols I will cleanse you. I will give you a new heart and place a new spirit within you, taking from your bodies your stony hearts and giving you natural hearts. I will put my spirit within you and make you live by my statutes, careful to observe my decrees. You shall live in the land I gave your fathers; you shall be my people, and I will be your God.

(parallel passage from Jeremiah)
I will be their God, and they shall be my people

Jer 31:31-34; 32:37-41

The days are coming, says the Lord, when I will make a
new covenant with the house of Israel and the house of
Judah. It will not be like the covenant I made with their
fathers the day I took them by the hand to lead them
forth from the land of Egypt; for they broke my
covenant, and I had to show myself their master, says
the Lord. But this is the covenant which I will make with
the house of Israel after those days, says the Lord. I will
place my law within them, and write it upon their
hearts; I will be their God, and they shall be my people.
No longer will they have need to teach their friends and
kinsmen how to know the Lord. All, from least to
greatest, shall know me, says the Lord, for I will forgive
their evildoing and remember their sin no more.

Behold, I will gather them together from all the lands
to which in anger, wrath, and great rage I banish them;
I will bring them back to this place and settle them here
in safety. They shall be my people, and I will be their
God. One heart and one way I will give them, that they
may fear me always, to their own good and that of their
children after them. I will make with them an eternal
covenant, never to cease doing good to them; into their
hearts I will put the fear of me, that they may never
depart from me. I will take delight in doing good to
them: I will replant them firmly in this land, with all
my heart and soul.

THE DRY BONES

I will put my spirit in you that you may live . . .

Ez 37:1-14

The hand of the Lord came upon me and he led me out
in the spirit of the Lord and set me in the center of the
plain, which was now filled with bones. He made me
walk among them in every direction so that I saw how
many they were on the surface of the plain. How dry
they were! He asked me: Son of man, can these bones
come to life? "Lord God," I answered, "you alone know
that." Then he said to me: Prophesy over these
bones, and say to them: Dry bones, hear the word of
the Lord. Thus says the Lord God to these bones:
See! I will bring spirit into you, that you may come
to life. I will put sinews upon you, make flesh grow
over you, cover you with skin, and put spirit in you
so that you may come to life and know that I am the
Lord. I prophesied as I had been told, and even as I
was prophesying I heard a noise; it was a rattling as
the bones came together, bone joining bone. I saw the
sinews and the flesh come upon them, and the skin cover
them, but there was no spirit in them. Then he said
to me: Prophesy to the spirit, prophesy, son of man,
and say to the spirit: Thus says the Lord God: From
the four winds come, O spirit, and breathe into these
slain that they may come to life. I prophesied as he

told me, and the spirit came into them; they came alive and stood upright, a vast army. Then he said to me: Son of man, these bones are the whole house of Israel. They have been saying, "Our bones are dried up, our hope is lost, and we are cut off." Therefore, prophesy and say to them: Thus says the Lord God: O my people, I will open your graves and have you rise from them, and bring you back to the land of Israel. Then you shall know that I am the Lord, when I open your graves and have you rise from them. O my people! I will put my spirit in you that you may live, and I will settle you upon your land; thus you shall know that I am the Lord. I have promised, and I will do it, says the Lord.

A PROMISE TO ISRAEL

I have poured out my spirit upon the house of Israel . . .

Ez 39:27-29

When I bring them back from among the peoples, I will gather them from the lands of their enemies, and will prove my holiness through them in the sight of many nations. Thus they shall know that I, the Lord, am their God, since I, who exiled them among the nations, will gather them back on their land, not leaving any of them behind. No longer will I hide my face from them, for I have poured out my spirit upon the house of Israel, says the Lord God.

THE RETURN OF THE LORD

. . . the spirit lifted me up and brought me to the inner court

Ez 43:1-8

Then he led me to the gate which faces the east, and there I saw the glory of the God of Israel coming from the east. I heard a sound like the roaring of many waters, and the earth shone with his glory. The vision was like that which I had seen when he came to destroy the city, and like that which I had seen by the river Chebar. I fell prone as the glory of the Lord entered the temple by way of the gate which faces the east, but (the) spirit lifted me up and brought me to the inner court. And I saw that the temple was filled with the glory of the Lord. Then I heard someone speaking to me from the temple, while the man stood beside me. The voice said to me: Son of man, this is where my throne shall be, this is where I will set the soles of my feet; here I will dwell among the Israelites forever.

DANIEL

. . . in whom is the spirit of the holy God

Dn 4:1-15

I, Nebuchadnezzar, was at home in my palace, content and prosperous. I had a terrifying dream as I lay in bed, and the images and visions of my mind frightened me. So I issued a decree that all the wise men of Babylon should be brought before me to give the interpretation of the dream. When the magicians, enchanters, Chaldeans and astrologers had come in, I related the dream before them; but none of them could tell me its meaning. Finally there came before me Daniel, whose name is Belteshazzar after the name of my god, and in whom is the spirit of the holy God. I repeated the dream to him: "Belteshazzar, chief of the magicians, I know that the spirit of the holy God is in you and no mystery is too difficult for you; tell me the meaning of the visions that I saw in my dream.

"These were the visions I saw while in bed: I saw a tree of great height at the center of the world. It was large and strong, with its top touching the heavens, and it could be seen to the ends of the earth. Its leaves were beautiful and its fruit abundant, providing food for all. Under it the wild beasts found shade, in its branches the birds of the air nested; all men ate of it. In the vision I saw while in bed, a holy sentinel came down from heaven, and cried out:

" 'Cut down the tree and lop off its branches,
     strip off its leaves and scatter its fruit;
     let the beasts flee its shade, and the birds its
     branches.
But leave in the earth its stump and roots,
     fettered with iron and bronze, in the grass of the
     field.
Let him be bathed with the dew of heaven;
     his lot be to eat, among beasts, the grass of the
     earth.
Let his mind be changed from the human;
     let him be given the sense of a beast,
     till seven years pass over him.
By decree of the sentinels is this decided,
     by order of the holy ones, this sentence;

That all who live may know
   that the Most High rules over the kingdom of
   men:
He can give it to whom he will,
   or set over it the lowliest of men.'

"This is the dream that I, King Nebuchadnezzar, had.
Now, Belteshazzar, tell me its meaning. Although none
of the wise men in my kingdom can tell me the meaning,
you can, because the spirit of the holy God is in you."

Then Daniel, whose name was Belteshazzar, was
appalled for a while, terrified by his thoughts. "Belteshazzar," the king said to him, "let not the dream or its
meaning terrify you." "My lord," Belteshazzar replied,
"this dream should be for your enemies, and its meaning
for your foes. The large, strong tree that you saw, with
its top touching the heavens, that could be seen by the
whole earth, which had beautiful foliage and abundant
fruit, providing food for all, under which the wild beasts
lived, and in whose branches the birds of the air dwelt—
you are that tree, O king, large and strong! Your majesty
has become so great as to touch the heavens, and your
rule extends over the whole earth. As for the king's
vision of a holy sentinel that came down from heaven
and proclaimed: 'Cut down the tree and destroy it, but
leave in the earth its stump and roots, fettered with
iron and bronze in the grass of the field; let him be
bathed with the dew of heaven and let his lot be among
wild beasts till seven years pass over him'—this is its
meaning, O king; this is the sentence which the Most
High has passed upon my lord king: You shall be cast
out from among men and dwell with wild beasts; you
shall be given grass to eat like an ox and be bathed with
the dew of heaven; seven years shall pass over you,

until you know that the Most High rules over the kingdom of men and gives it to whom he will. The command that the stump and roots of the tree are to be left means that your kingdom shall be preserved for you, once you have learned it is heaven that rules. Therefore, O king, take my advice; atone for your sins by good deeds, and for your misdeeds by kindness to the poor; then your prosperity will be long."

JOEL

THE OUTPOURING OF THE SPIRIT

. . . I will pour out my spirit on all mankind

Jl 3:1-5

Then afterward I will pour out
    my spirit upon all mankind.
Your sons and daughters shall prophesy,
    your old men shall dream dreams,
    your young men shall see visions;
Even upon the servants and the handmaids,
    in those days, I will pour out my spirit.

And I will work wonders in the
    heavens and on the earth,
    blood, fire, and columns of smoke;
The sun will be turned to darkness,
    and the moon to blood,
At the coming of the day of the Lord,
    the great and terrible day.
Then everyone shall be rescued
    who calls on the name of the Lord;

For on Mount Zion there shall be a remnant,
    as the Lord has said,
And in Jerusalem survivors
    whom the Lord shall call.

MICAH

I am filled . . . with the spirit of the Lord . . .

Mi 3:8-10, 12

But as for me, I am filled with power,
    with the spirit of the Lord,
    with authority and with might;
To declare to Jacob his crimes
    and to Israel his sins.
Hear this, you leaders of the house of Jacob,
    you rulers of the house of Israel!
You who abhor what is just,
    and pervert all that is right;
Who build up Zion with bloodshed,
    and Jerusalem with wickedness! . . .
Therefore, because of you,
    Zion shall be plowed like a field,
    and Jerusalem reduced to rubble,
And the mount of the temple
    to a forest ridge.

HAGGAI

FUTURE GLORY OF THE NEW TEMPLE

. . . my spirit continues in your midst

Hg 1:14, 2:1-9

Then the Lord stirred up the spirit of the governor
of Judah, Zerubbabel, son of Shealtiel, and the spirit
of the high priest Joshua, son of Jehozadak, and the
spirit of all the remnant of the people, so that they
came and set to work on the house of the Lord of hosts.

In the second year of King Darius, on the twenty-first
day of the seventh month, the word of the Lord came
through the prophet Haggai: Tell this to the governor
of Judah, Zerubbabel, son of Shealtiel, and to the high
priest Joshua, son of Jehozadak, and to the remnant
of the people,

> Who is left among you
>> that saw this house in its former glory?
> And how do you see it now?
>> Does it not seem like nothing in your eyes?
> But now take courage, Zerubbabel, says the Lord,
>> and take courage, Joshua, high priest,
>>> son of Jehozadak,
>> And take courage, all you people of the land,
>> says the Lord, and work!
>> For I am with you, says the Lord of hosts.
> This is the pact that I made with you
>> when you came out of Egypt,
> And my spirit continues in your midst;
>> do not fear!

For thus says the Lord of hosts:
One moment yet, a little while,
    and I will shake the heavens and the earth,
    the sea and the dry land.
I will shake all the nations,
    and the treasures of all the nations will come in,
And I will fill this house with glory,
    says the Lord of hosts.
Mine is the silver and mine the gold,
    says the Lord of hosts.
Greater will be the future glory of this house
    than the former, says the Lord of hosts;
And in this place I will give peace,
    says the Lord of hosts!

ZECHARIAH

THE REBUILDING OF THE TEMPLE

Not by an army, nor by might, but by my spirit . . .

Zec 4:6-10

Then he said to me, "This is the Lord's message to
Zerubbabel: Not by an army, nor by might, but by my
spirit, says the Lord of hosts. What are you, O great
mountain? Before Zerubbabel you are but a plain.
He shall bring out the capstone amid exclamations of
'Hail, Hail' to it."

This word of the Lord came to me: the hands of
Zerubbabel have laid the foundations of this house, and
his hands shall finish it; then you shall know that the
Lord of hosts has sent me to you. For even they who

were scornful on that day of small beginnings shall rejoice to see the select stone in the hands of Zerubbabel.

MESSIANIC JERUSALEM

I will pour out . . . a spirit of grace and petition

Zec 12:10

I will pour out on the house of David and on the inhabitants of Jerusalem a spirit of grace and petition; and they shall look on him whom they have thrust through, and they shall mourn for him as one mourns for an only son, and they shall grieve over him as one grieves over a first-born.

PART II

THE SPIRIT IN
THE GOSPELS

1. The Outpouring of the Spirit at the Birth of John and Jesus

ANNOUNCEMENT OF THE BIRTH OF JOHN

. . . and he will be filled with the Holy Spirit from his mother's womb

Lk 1:5-17

In the days of Herod, king of Judea, there was a priest named Zechariah of the priestly class of Abijah; his wife was a descendant of Aaron named Elizabeth. Both were just in the eyes of God, blamelessly following all the commandments and ordinances of the Lord. They were childless, for Elizabeth was sterile; moreover, both were advanced in years.

Once, when it was the turn of Zechariah's class and he was fulfilling his functions as a priest before God, it fell to him by lot according to priestly usage to enter the sanctuary of the Lord and offer incense. While the full assembly of people was praying outside at the incense hour, an angel of the Lord appeared to him, standing at the right of the altar of incense. Zechariah was deeply disturbed upon seeing him, and overcome by fear.

The angel said to him: "Do not be frightened, Zechariah, your prayer has been heard. Your wife

Elizabeth shall bear a son whom you shall name John.
Joy and gladness will be yours, and many will rejoice at
his birth; for he will be great in the eyes of the Lord.
He will never drink wine or strong drink, and he will be
filled with the Holy Spirit from his mother's womb.
Many of the sons of Israel will he bring back to the
Lord their God. God himself will go before him, in the
spirit and power of Elijah, to turn the hearts of fathers
to their children and the rebellious to the wisdom of the
just, and to prepare for the Lord a people well-disposed."

ANNOUNCEMENT OF THE BIRTH OF JESUS

The Holy Spirit will come upon you . . .

Lk 1:26-38

In the sixth month, the angel Gabriel was sent from God
to a town of Galilee named Nazareth, to a virgin
betrothed to a man named Joseph, of the house of David.
The virgin's name was Mary. Upon arriving, the angel
said to her: "Rejoice, O highly favored daughter! The
Lord is with you. Blessed are you among women." She
was deeply troubled by his words, and wondered what
his greeting meant. The angel went on to say to her:
"Do not fear, Mary. You have found favor with God.
You shall conceive and bear a son and give him the
name Jesus. Great will be his dignity and he will be
called Son of the Most High. The Lord God will give
him the throne of David his father. He will rule over
the house of Jacob forever and his reign will be without
end."

Mary said to the angel, "How can this be since I
do not know man?" The angel answered her: "The Holy

Spirit will come upon you and the power of the Most
High will overshadow you; hence, the holy offspring to
be born will be called Son of God. Know that Elizabeth
your kinswoman has conceived a son in her old age;
she who was thought to be sterile is now in her sixth
month, for nothing is impossible with God."

Mary said: "I am the servant of the Lord. Let it be
done to me as you say." With that the angel left her.

MARY VISITS ELIZABETH

Elizabeth was filled with the Holy Spirit . . .

Lk 1:39-56

Thereupon Mary set out, proceeding in haste into the
hill country to a town of Judah, where she entered
Zechariah's house and greeted Elizabeth. When Elizabeth
heard Mary's greeting, the baby leapt in her womb.
Elizabeth was filled with the Holy Spirit and cried out in
a loud voice: "Blest are you among women and blest
is the fruit of your womb. But who am I that the mother
of my Lord should come to me? The moment your
greeting sounded in my ears, the baby leapt in my womb
for joy. Blest is she who trusted that the Lord's words
to her would be fulfilled."

Mary's Canticle
Then Mary said:

"My being proclaims the greatness of the Lord,
    my spirit finds joy in God my savior,
For he has looked upon his servant in her lowliness;
    all ages to come shall call me blessed.

God who is mighty has done great things for me,
> holy is his name;
His mercy is from age to age on those who fear him.

"He has shown might with his arm;
> he has confused the proud in their inmost
>   thoughts.
He has deposed the mighty from their thrones
> and raised the lowly to high places.
The hungry he has given every good thing,
> while the rich he has sent empty away.
He has upheld Israel his servant,
> ever mindful of his mercy;
Even as he promised our fathers, promised
> Abraham and his descendants forever."

Mary remained with Elizabeth about three months and then returned home.

THE BIRTH OF JOHN THE BAPTIST

Zechariah, filled with the Holy Spirit, uttered this prophecy . . .

Lk 1:57-80

When Elizabeth's time for delivery arrived, she gave birth to a son. Her neighbors and relatives, upon hearing that the Lord had extended his mercy to her, rejoiced with her. When they assembled for the circumcision of the child on the eighth day, they intended to name him after his father Zechariah. At this his mother intervened, saying, "No, he is to be called John."

They pointed out to her, "None of your relatives has this name."

Then, using signs, they asked the father what he wished him to be called.

He signaled for a writing tablet and wrote the words, "His name is John." This astonished them all. At that moment his mouth was opened and his tongue loosed, and he began to speak in praise of God.

Fear descended on all in the neighborhood; throughout the hill country of Judea these happenings began to be recounted to the last detail. All who heard stored these things up in their hearts, saying, "What will this child be?" and, "Was not the hand of the Lord upon him?"

Zechariah's Canticle

Then Zechariah his father, filled with the Holy Spirit, uttered this prophecy:

Blessed be the Lord the God of Israel
   because he has visited and ransomed his people.
He has raised a horn of saving strength for us
   in the house of David his servant,
As he promised through the mouths of his holy ones,
   the prophets of ancient times:
Salvation from our enemies
   and from the hands of all our foes.
He has dealt mercifully with our fathers
   and remembered the holy covenant he made,
The oath he swore to Abraham our father he would
      grant us:
   that, rid of fear and delivered from the enemy,
We should serve him devoutly and through all our
      days
   be holy in his sight.

And you, O child, shall be called
    prophet of the Most High;
For you shall go before the Lord
    to prepare straight paths for him,
Giving his people a knowledge of salvation
    in freedom from their sins.
All this is the work of the kindness of our God;
    he, the Dayspring, shall visit us in his mercy
To shine on those who sit in darkness and in the
        shadow of death,
    to guide our feet into the way of peace."

The child grew up and matured in spirit. He lived in the desert until the day when he made his public appearance in Israel.

THE BIRTH OF JESUS

It is by the Holy Spirit that she has conceived this child

Mt 1:18-23

Now this is how the birth of Jesus Christ came about. When his mother Mary was engaged to Joseph, but before they lived together, she was found with child through the power of the Holy Spirit. Joseph her husband, an upright man unwilling to expose her to the law, decided to divorce her quietly. Such was his intention when suddenly the angel of the Lord appeared in a dream and said to him: "Joseph, son of David, have no fear about taking Mary as your wife. It is by the Holy Spirit that she has conceived this child. She is to have a son and you are to name him Jesus because he will save his people from their sins."

All this happened to fulfill what the Lord had said
   through the prophet:

"The virgin shall be with child and give birth to a son,
   and they shall call him Emmanuel,"

a name which means "God is with us." When Joseph
awoke he did as the angel of the Lord had directed him
and received her into his home as his wife. He had
no relations with her at any time before she bore a son,
whom he named Jesus.

SIMEON

*He came to the temple, now, inspired by the Holy
Spirit . . .*

Lk 2:22-35

When the day came to purify them according to the law
of Moses, the couple brought him up to Jerusalem so
that he could be presented to the Lord, for it is written
in the law of the Lord, "Every first-born male shall be
consecrated to the Lord." They came to offer in sacrifice
"a pair of turtledoves or two young pigeons," in accord
with the dictate in the law of the Lord.

There lived in Jerusalem at the time a certain man
named Simeon. He was just and pious, and awaited the
consolation of Israel, and the Holy Spirit was upon him.
It was revealed to him by the Holy Spirit that he would
not experience death until he had seen the Anointed of
the Lord. He came to the temple, now, inspired by the
Spirit, and when the parents brought in the child Jesus
to perform for him the customary ritual of the law,
he took him in his arms and blessed God in these words:

"Now, Master, you can dismiss your servant in peace;
    you have fulfilled your word.
For my eyes have witnessed your saving deed
    displayed for all the peoples to see:
A revealing light to the Gentiles,
    the glory of your people Israel."

The child's father and mother were marveling at
what was being said about him. Simeon blessed them
and said to Mary his mother: "This child is destined to
be the downfall and the rise of many in Israel, a sign
that will be opposed—and you yourself shall be pierced
with a sword—so that the thoughts of many hearts may
be laid bare."

ANNA

There was also a certain prophetess . . .

Lk 2:36-38

There was also a certain prophetess, Anna by name,
daughter of Phanuel of the tribe of Asher. She had
seen many days, having lived seven years with her
husband after her marriage and then as a widow until
she was eighty-four. She was constantly in the temple,
worshiping day and night in fasting and prayer. Coming
on the scene at this moment, she gave thanks to God
and talked about the child to all who looked forward
to the deliverance of Jerusalem.

When the pair had fulfilled all the prescriptions of
the law of the Lord, they returned to Galilee and their
own town of Nazareth. The child grew in size and
strength, filled with wisdom, and the grace of God was
upon him.

2. The Preaching of John about Jesus

. . . he will baptize you with the Holy Spirit and with fire

Mt 3:7-12

When John the Baptizer made his appearance as a
preacher in the desert of Judea, this was his theme:
"Reform your lives! The reign of God is at hand." It
was of him that the prophet Isaiah had spoken when he
said:

> "A herald's voice in the desert: 'Prepare the way of
> the Lord, make straight his paths.' "

John was clothed in a garment of camel's hair, and
wore a leather belt around his waist. Grasshoppers and
wild honey were his food. At that time Jerusalem, all
Judea, and the whole region around the Jordan were
going out to him. They were being baptized by him in
the Jordan River as they confessed their sins.

When he saw that many of the Pharisees and Sadducees were stepping forward for this bath, he said to
them: "You brood of vipers! Who told you to flee from
the wrath to come? Give some evidence that you mean
to reform. Do not pride yourselves on the claim,
'Abraham is our father.' I tell you, God can raise up

children to Abraham from these very stones. Even now the ax is laid to the root of the tree. Every tree that is not fruitful will be cut down and thrown into the fire. I baptize you in water for the sake of reform, but the one who will follow me is more powerful than I. I am not even fit to carry his sandals. He it is who will baptize you in the Holy Spirit and fire. His winnowing-fan is in his hand. He will clear the threshing floor and gather his grain into the barn, but the chaff he will burn in unquenchable fire."

. . . he will baptize you in the Holy Spirit

Mk 1:1-8

Here begins the gospel of Jesus Christ, the Son of God. In Isaiah the prophet it is written:

"I send my messenger before you to prepare your
way:
a herald's voice in the desert, crying,
'Make ready the way of the Lord,
clear him a straight path.' "

Thus it was that John the Baptizer appeared in the desert, proclaiming a baptism of repentance which led to the forgiveness of sins. All the Judean countryside and the people of Jerusalem went out to him in great numbers. They were being baptized by him in the Jordan River as they confessed their sins. John was clothed in camel's hair, and wore a leather belt around his waist. His food was grasshoppers and wild honey. The theme of his preaching was: "One more powerful than I is to come after me. I am not fit to stoop and untie his sandal straps. I have baptized you in water; he will baptize you in the Holy Spirit."

he will baptize you in the Holy Spirit and in fire

Lk 3:15-18

The people were full of anticipation, wondering in their hearts whether John might be the Messiah. John answered them all by saying: "I am baptizing you in water, but there is one to come who is mightier than I. I am not fit to loosen his sandal strap. He will baptize you in the Holy Spirit and in fire. His winnowing-fan is in his hand to clear his threshing floor and gather the wheat into his barn; but the chaff he will burn in unquenchable fire." Using exhortations of this sort, he preached the good news to the people.

3. The Baptism of Jesus

. . . he saw the Spirit of God descend like a dove . . .

Mt 3:13-17

Later Jesus, coming from Galilee, appeared before John
at the Jordan to be baptized by him. John tried to
refuse him with the protest, "I should be baptized by
you, yet you come to me!" Jesus answered: "Give in for
now. We must do this if we would fulfill all of God's
demands." So John gave in. After Jesus was baptized,
he came directly out of the water. Suddenly the sky
opened and he saw the Spirit of God descend like a dove
and hover over him. With that, a voice from the
heavens said, "This is my beloved Son. My favor rests
on him."

*. . . he saw the sky rent in two and the Spirit descending
on him . . .*

Mk 1:9-11

During that time, Jesus came from Nazareth in Galilee
and was baptized in the Jordan by John. Immediately
on coming up out of the water he saw the sky rent in
two and the Spirit descending on him like a dove. Then

a voice came from the heavens: "You are my beloved
Son. On you my favor rests."

. . . the Holy Spirit descended on him . . .

Lk 3:21-22

When all the people were baptized, and Jesus was at
prayer after likewise being baptized, the skies opened
and the Holy Spirit descended on him in visible form
like a dove. A voice from heaven was heard to say:
"You are my beloved Son. On you my favor rests."

I saw the Spirit descend . . . and it came to rest on him

Jn 1:29-34

The next day, when John caught sight of Jesus coming
toward him, he exclaimed:

> "Look! There is the Lamb of God
> who takes away the sin of the world!

It is he of whom I said:

> 'After me is to come a man who ranks ahead of me,
> because he was before me.'

I confess I did not recognize him, though the very
reason I came baptizing with water was that he might
be revealed to Israel."
John gave this testimony also:

> "I saw the Spirit descend like a dove from the sky,

and it came to rest on him.

But I did not recognize him. The one who sent me to baptize with water told me, 'When you see the Spirit descend and rest on someone, it is he who is to baptize with the Holy Spirit.' Now I have seen for myself and have testified, 'This is God's chosen One.' "

4. The Temptation of Jesus

Then Jesus was led into the desert by the Spirit . . .

Mt 4:1-11

Then Jesus was led into the desert by the Spirit to be
tempted by the devil. He fasted forty days and forty
nights, and afterward was hungry. The tempter ap-
proached and said to him, "If you are the Son of God,
command these stones to turn into bread." Jesus replied,
"Scripture has it:

> 'Not on bread alone is man to live
> but on every utterance that comes from the mouth
> of God.' "

Next the devil took him to the holy city, set him on
the parapet of the temple, and said, "If you are the
Son of God, throw yourself down. Scripture has it:

> 'He will bid his angels take care of you;
> with their hands they will support you
> that you may never stumble on a stone.' "

Jesus answered him, "Scripture also has it:

> 'You shall not put the Lord your God to the test.' "

The devil then took him up a very high mountain and displayed before him all the kingdoms of the world in their magnificence, promising, "All these will I bestow on you if you prostrate yourself in homage before me." At this, Jesus said to him, "Away with you, Satan! Scripture has it:

'You shall do homage to the Lord your God;
him alone shall you adore.' "

At that the devil left him, and angels came and waited on him.

At that point the Spirit sent him out toward the desert

Mk 1:12-13

At that point the Spirit sent him out toward the desert. He stayed in the wasteland forty days, put to the test there by Satan. He was with the wild beasts, and angels waited on him.

Jesus, full of the Spirit . . . was conducted by the Spirit into the desert . . .

Lk 4:1-13

Jesus, full of the Holy Spirit, then returned from the Jordan and was conducted by the Spirit into the desert for forty days, where he was tempted by the devil. During that time he ate nothing, and at the end of it he was hungry. The devil said to him, "If you are the Son of God, command this stone to turn into bread." Jesus answered him, "Scripture has it, 'Not on bread alone shall man live.' "

Then the devil took him up higher and showed him all the kingdoms of the world in a single instant. He said to him, "I will give you all this power and the glory of these kingdoms; the power has been given to me and I give it to whomever I wish. Prostrate yourself in homage before me, and it shall all be yours." In reply, Jesus said to him, "Scripture has it,

'You shall do homage to the Lord your God;
   him alone shall you adore.' "

Then the devil led him to Jerusalem, set him on the parapet of the temple, and said to him, "If you are the Son of God, throw yourself down from here, for Scripture has it,

'He will bid his angels watch over you';

and again,

'With their hands they will support you,
   that you may never stumble on a stone.' "

Jesus said to him in reply, "It also says, 'You shall not put the Lord your God to the test.' "
   When the devil had finished all the tempting he left him, to await another opportunity.

5. Jesus Begins His Work

Jesus returned in the power of the Spirit to Galilee . . .

Lk 4:14-15

Jesus returned in the power of the Spirit to Galilee, and his reputation spread throughout the region. He was teaching in their synagogues, and all were loud in his praise.

JESUS REJECTED AT NAZARETH

The Spirit of the Lord is upon me

Lk 4:16-22

He came to Nazareth where he had been reared, and entering the synagogue on the sabbath as he was in the habit of doing, he stood up to do the reading. When the book of the prophet Isaiah was handed him, he unrolled the scroll and found the passage where it was written:

"The spirit of the Lord is upon me;
    therefore he has anointed me.
He has sent me to bring glad tidings to the poor,
    to proclaim liberty to captives,

Recovery of sight to the blind and release to prisoners,
To announce a year of favor from the Lord."

Rolling up the scroll he gave it back to the assistant and
sat down. All in the synagogue had their eyes fixed on
him. Then he began by saying to them, "Today this
Scripture passage is fulfilled in your hearing." All who
were present spoke favorably of him; they marveled at
the appealing discourse which came from his lips. They
also asked, "Is not this Joseph's son?"

JESUS REJOICES

At that moment Jesus rejoiced in the Holy Spirit . . .

Lk 10:21-24

At that moment Jesus rejoiced in the Holy Spirit and
said: "I offer you praise, O Father, Lord of heaven and
earth, because what you have hidden from the learned
and the clever you have revealed to the merest children.
    "Yes, Father, you have graciously willed it so.
Everything has been given over to me by my Father. No
one knows the Son except the Father and no one knows
the Father except the Son—and anyone to whom the
Son wishes to reveal him."
    Turning to his disciples he said to them privately:
"Blest are the eyes that see what you see. I tell you,
many prophets and kings wished to see what you see but
did not see it, and to hear what you hear but did not
hear it."

JESUS' TEACHING ON PRAYER

. . . how much more will your heavenly Father give good things . . . !

Mt 6:6-13; 7:7-11

"When you are praying, do not behave like the hypocrites who love to stand and pray in synagogues or on street corners in order to be noticed. I give you my word, they are already repaid. Whenever you pray, go to your room, close your door, and pray to your Father in private. Then your Father, who sees what no man sees, will repay you. In your prayer do not rattle on like the pagans. They think they will win a hearing by the sheer multiplication of words. Do not imitate them. Your Father knows what you need before you ask him. This is how you are to pray:

'Our Father in heaven,
hallowed be your name,
your kingdom come,
your will be done
on earth as it is in heaven.
Give us today our daily bread,
and forgive us the wrong we have done
as we forgive those who wrong us.
Subject us not to the trial
but deliver us from the evil one.'

"If you forgive the faults of others, your heavenly Father will forgive you yours. If you do not forgive others, neither will your Father forgive you."

"Ask, and you will receive. Seek, and you will find. Knock, and it will be opened to you. For the one who asks, receives. The one who seeks, finds. The one who knocks, enters. Would one of you hand his son a stone when he asks for a loaf, or a poisonous snake when he asks for a fish? If you, with all your sins, know how to give your children what is good, how much more will your heavenly Father give good things* to anyone who asks him!"

. . . how much more will the heavenly Father give the Holy Spirit . . .

Lk 11:1-13

One day he was praying in a certain place. When he had finished, one of his disciples asked him, "Lord, teach us to pray, as John taught his disciples." He said to them, "When you pray, say:

> 'Father,
> hallowed be your name,
> your kingdom come.
> Give us each day our daily bread.
> Forgive us our sins
> for we too forgive all who do us wrong;
> and subject us not to the trial.' "

Jesus said to them: "If one of you knows someone who comes to him in the middle of the night and says to him, 'Friend, lend me three loaves, for a friend of mine has

---

*"Good things" are identified as the "Holy Spirit" in Lk 11:13, p. 88

87

come in from a journey and I have nothing to offer him';
and he from inside should reply, 'Leave me alone. The
door is shut now and my children and I are in bed.
I cannot get up to look after your needs'—I tell you,
even though he does not get up and take care of the man
because of friendship, he will do so because of his
persistence, and give him as much as he needs.

"So I say to you, 'Ask and you shall receive; seek and
you shall find; knock and it shall be opened to you.'

"For whoever asks, receives; whoever seeks, finds;
whoever knocks, is admitted. What father among you
will give his son a snake if he asks for a fish, or hand
him a scorpion if he asks for an egg? If you, with all
your sins, know how to give your children good things,
how much more will the heavenly Father give the Holy
Spirit to those who ask him."

MY CHOSEN SERVANT

I will endow him with my spirit . . .

Mt 12:9-21

He left that place and went into their synagogue. A man
with a shriveled hand happened to be there, and they put
this question to Jesus, hoping to bring an accusation
against him: "Is it lawful to work a cure on the sabbath?"
He said in response: "Suppose one of you has a sheep
and it falls into a pit on the sabbath. Will he not take
hold of it and pull it out? Well, think how much more
precious a human being is than a sheep. Clearly, good
deeds may be performed on the sabbath."

To the man he said, "Stretch out your hand." He did
so, and it was perfectly restored; it became as sound as
the other. When the Pharisees were outside they began to

plot against him to find a way to destroy him. Jesus was aware of this, and so he withdrew from that place.

Many people followed him and he cured them all, though he sternly ordered them not to make public what he had done. This was to fulfill what had been said through Isaiah the prophet:

> "Here is my servant whom I have chosen,
> my loved one in whom I delight.
> I will endow him with my spirit*
> and he will proclaim justice to the Gentiles.
> He will not contend or cry out,
> nor will his voice be heard in the streets.
> The bruised reed he will not crush;
> the smoldering wick he will not quench
> until judgment is made victorious.
> In his name, the Gentiles will find hope."

---

*RSV reads: I will put my Spirit upon him . . .

6. Jesus and Beelzebul

. . . it is by the Spirit of God that I expel demons . . .

Mt 12:22-32

A possessed man who was brought to him was blind
and mute. He cured the man so that he could speak and
see. All in the crowd were astonished. "Might this not be
David's son?" they asked. When the Pharisees heard this,
they charged, "This man can expel demons only with
the help of Beelzebul, the prince of demons." Knowing
their thoughts, he said to them: "A kingdom torn by
strife is headed for its downfall. A town or household
split into factions cannot last long. If Satan is expelling
Satan, he must be torn by dissension. How, then, can his
dominion last? If I expel demons with Beelzebul's help,
by whose help do your people expel them? Let them be
the ones to judge you. But if it is by the Spirit of God
that I expel demons, then the reign of God has overtaken
you.

"How can anyone enter a strong man's house and
make off with his property unless he first ties him
securely? Only then can he rob his house. He who is not
with me is against me, and he who does not gather with
me scatters.

"That, I assure you, is why every sin, every
blasphemy, will be forgiven men, but blasphemy against
the Spirit will not be forgiven. Whoever says anything

against the Son of Man will be forgiven, but whoever says anything against the Holy Spirit will not be forgiven, either in this age or in the age to come. Declare a tree good and its fruit good or declare a tree rotten and its fruit rotten, one or the other, for you can tell a tree by its fruit."

. . . whoever blasphemes against the Holy Spirit will never be forgiven

Mk 3:20-30

He returned to the house with them and again the crowd assembled, making it impossible for them to get any food whatever. When his family heard of this they came to take charge of him, saying, "He is out of his mind"; while the scribes who arrived from Jerusalem asserted, "He is possessed by Beelzebul," and "He expels demons with the help of the prince of demons." Summoning them, he then began to speak to them by way of examples: "How can Satan expel Satan? If a kingdom is torn by civil strife, that kingdom cannot last. If a household is divided according to loyalties, that household will not survive. Similarly, if Satan has suffered mutiny in his ranks and is torn by dissension, he cannot endure; he is finished. No one can enter a strong man's house and despoil his property unless he has first put him under restraint. Only then can he plunder his house.

"I give you my word, every sin will be forgiven mankind and all the blasphemies men utter, but whoever blasphemes against the Holy Spirit will never be forgiven. He carries the guilt of his sin without end." He spoke thus because they had said, "He is possessed by an unclean spirit."

. . . if it is by the finger of God that I cast out devils . . .

Lk 11:14-20

Jesus was casting out a devil which was mute, and when the devil was cast out the dumb man spoke. The crowds were amazed at this. Some of them said, "It is by Beelzebul, the prince of devils, that he casts out devils." Others, to test him, were demanding of him a sign from heaven.

Because he knew their thoughts, he said to them: "Every kingdom divided against itself is laid waste. Any house torn by dissension falls. If Satan is divided against himself, how can his kingdom last?—since you say it is by Beelzebul that I cast out devils. If I cast out devils by Beelzebul, by whom do your people cast them out? In such case, let them act as your judges. But if it is by the finger of God* that I cast out devils, then the reign of God is upon you.

"When a strong man fully armed guards his courtyard, his possessions go undisturbed. But when someone stronger than he comes and overpowers him, such a one carries off the arms on which he was relying and divides the spoils. He who is not with me is against me, and he who does not gather with me scatters.

"When an unclean spirit has gone out of a man, it wanders through arid wastes searching for a resting-place; failing to find one, it says, 'I will go back to where I came from.' It then returns, to find the house swept and tidied. Next it goes out and returns with seven other spirits far worse than itself, who enter in and dwell there. The result is that the last state of the man is worse than the first."

---

*Matthew reads: . . . by the Spirit of God . . . , see p. 90

7. Coming Persecutions

. . . the Spirit of your Father will be speaking in you

Mt 10:16-20

"What I am doing is sending you out like sheep among wolves. You must be clever as snakes and innocent as doves. Be on your guard with respect to others. They will hale you into court, they will flog you in their synagogues. You will be brought to trial before rulers and kings, to give witness before them and before the Gentiles on my account. When they hand you over, do not worry about what you will say or how you will say it. When the hour comes, you will be given what you are to say. You yourselves will not be the speakers; the Spirit of your Father will be speaking in you.

It will not be yourselves speaking but the Holy Spirit

Mk 13:9-13

Be constantly on your guard. They will hand you over to the courts. You will be beaten in synagogues. You will be arraigned before governors and kings on my account and have to testify to your faith before them. But the

93

good news must first be proclaimed to all the Gentiles. When men take you off into custody, do not worry beforehand about what to say. In that hour, say what you are inspired to say. It will not be yourselves speaking but the Holy Spirit. Brother will hand over brother for execution and likewise the father his child; children will turn against their parents and have them put to death. Because of my name, you will be hated by everyone. Nonetheless, the man who holds out till the end is the one who will come through safe.

The Holy Spirit will teach you at that moment all that should be said

Lk 12:8-12

"I tell you, whoever acknowledges me before men—the Son of Man will acknowledge him before the angels of God. But the man who has disowned me in the presence of men will be disowned in the presence of the angels of God. Anyone who speaks against the Son of Man will be forgiven, but whoever blasphemes the Holy Spirit will never be forgiven. When they bring you before synagogues, rulers and authorities, do not worry about how to defend yourselves or what to say. The Holy Spirit will teach you at that moment all that should be said."

8. The Son of David Question

Then how is it that David under the Spirit's influence calls him "Lord" . . .

Mt 22:41-46

In turn Jesus put a question to the assembled Pharisees, "What is your opinion about the Messiah? Whose son is he?" "David's," they answered. He said to them, "Then how is it that David under the Spirit's influence calls him 'lord,' as he does:

'The Lord said to my lord, Sit at my right hand, until I humble your enemies beneath your feet'?

If David calls him 'lord,' how can he be his son?" No one could give him an answer; therefore no one dared, from that day on, to ask him any questions.

David himself, inspired by the Holy Spirit, said, "The Lord is my Lord" . . .

Mk 12:35-37

As Jesus was teaching in the temple precincts he went on

to say: "How can the scribes claim, 'The Messiah is David's son'? David himself, inspired by the Holy Spirit, said,

> 'The Lord said to my Lord: Sit at my right hand
> until I make your enemies your footstool.'

If David himself addresses him as 'Lord,' in what sense can he be his son?" The majority of the crowd heard this with delight.

9. The Spirit in John's Gospel

JESUS AND NICODEMUS

So it is with everyone begotten of the Spirit

Jn 3:1-8

A certain Pharisee named Nicodemus, a member of the
Jewish Sanhedrin, came to him at night. "Rabbi," he
said, "we know you are a teacher come from God, for no
man can perform signs and wonders such as you perform
unless God is with him." Jesus gave him this answer:

> "I solemnly assure you,
> no one can see the reign of God
> unless he is begotten from above."

"How can a man be born again once he is old?" retorted
Nicodemus. "Can he return to his mother's womb and be
born over again?" Jesus replied:

> "I solemnly assure you,
> no one can enter into God's kingdom
> without being begotten of water and Spirit.
> Flesh begets flesh,
> Spirit begets spirit.
> Do not be surprised that I tell you
> you must all be begotten from above.
> The wind blows where it will.
> You hear the sound it makes

but you do not know where it comes from, or where
    it goes.
So it is with everyone begotten of the Spirit."

. . . he does not ration his gift of the Spirit

Jn 3:31-36

"The One who comes from above is above all;
the one who is of the earth is earthly,
and he speaks on an earthly plane.
The One who comes from heaven [who is above all]
testifies to what he has seen and heard,
but no one accepts his testimony.
Whoever does accept this testimony
certifies that God is truthful.
For the One whom God has sent speaks the words of
    God; he does not ration his gift of the Spirit.
The Father loves the Son and has given everything over
    to him.

"Whoever believes in the Son has life eternal."

LIVING WATER

. . . he would have given you living water . . .

Jn 4:7-24

Now when Jesus learned that the Pharisees had heard
that he was winning over and baptizing more disciples
than John (in fact, however, it was not Jesus himself
who baptized, but his disciples), he left Judea and
started back for Galilee again.

He had to pass through Samaria, and his journey brought him to a Samaritan town named Shechem near the plot of land which Jacob had given to his son Joseph. This was the site of Jacob's well. Jesus, tired from his journey, sat down at the well.

The hour was about noon. When a Samaritan woman came to draw water, Jesus said to her, "Give me a drink." (His disciples had gone off to the town to buy provisions.) The Samaritan woman said to him, "You are a Jew. How can you ask me, a Samaritan and a woman, for a drink?" (Recall that Jews have nothing to do with Samaritans.) Jesus replied:

> "If only you recognized God's gift,
> and who it is that is asking you for a drink,
> you would have asked him instead,
> and he would have given you living water."*

"Sir," she challenged him, "You do not have a bucket and this well is deep. Where do you expect to get this flowing water? Surely you do not pretend to be greater than our ancestor Jacob, who gave us this well and drank from it with his sons and his flocks?" Jesus replied:

> "Everyone who drinks this water will be thirsty again.
> But whoever drinks the water I give him will never be thirsty;
> no, the water I give shall become a fountain within him,
> leaping up to provide eternal life."

The woman said to him, "Give me this water, sir, so that I shall not grow thirsty and have to keep coming here to draw water."

---

*On the identification of this "living water" as "the Spirit" see Jn 7:37-39, p. 102

God is Spirit, and those who worship him must worship him in spirit and in truth

He said to her, "Go, call your husband, and then come back here." "I have no husband," replied the woman. "You are right in saying you have no husband!" Jesus exclaimed. "The fact is, you have had five, and the man you are living with now is not your husband. What you said is true."

"Sir," answered the woman, "I can see you are a prophet. Our ancestors worshiped on this mountain, but you people claim that Jerusalem is the place where men ought to worship God." Jesus told her:

"Believe me, woman,
an hour is coming
when you will worship the Father
neither on this mountain
nor in Jerusalem.
You people worship what you do not understand,
while we understand what we worship;
after all, salvation is from the Jews.
Yet an hour is coming, and is already here,
when authentic worshipers
will worship the Father in Spirit and truth.
Indeed, it is just such worshipers the Father seeks.
God is Spirit,
and those who worship him
must worship in Spirit and truth."

The woman said to him: "I know there is a Messiah coming." (This term means Anointed.) "When he comes, he will tell us everything." Jesus replied, "I who speak to you am he."

WORDS OF ETERNAL LIFE

The words I spoke to you are spirit and life

Jn 6:60-69

After hearing his words, many of his disciples remarked, "This sort of talk is hard to endure! How can anyone take it seriously?" Jesus was fully aware that his disciples were murmuring in protest at what he had said. "Does it shake your faith?" he asked them.

> "What, then, if you were to see the Son of Man
> ascend to where he was before . . . ?
> It is the spirit that gives life; the flesh is useless.
> The words I spoke to you are spirit and life.
> Yet among you there are some who do not believe."

(Jesus knew from the start, of course, the ones who refused to believe, and the one who would hand him over.) He went on to say:

> "This is why I have told you that no one can come
>   to me unless it is granted him by the Father."

From this time on, many of his disciples broke away and would not remain in his company any longer. Jesus then said to the Twelve, "Do you want to leave me too?" Simon Peter answered him, "Lord, to whom shall we go? You have the words of eternal life. We have come to believe; we are convinced that you are God's holy one."

LIVING WATER
Second Episode

. . . rivers of living water . . . he was referring to the
Spirit . . .

Jn 7:37-39

On the last and greatest day of the festival, Jesus stood
up and cried out:

> "If anyone thirsts, let him come to me;
> let him drink who believes in me.
> Scripture has it:
> 'From within him rivers of living water shall flow.' "

(Here he was referring to the Spirit, whom those that
came to believe in him were to receive. There was, of
course, no Spirit as yet, since Jesus had not yet been
glorified.)

THE PROMISE OF THE HOLY SPIRIT

. . . another Paraclete to be with you always—the
Spirit of truth . . .

Jn 14:15-31

> "If you love me
> and obey the command I give you,
> I will ask the Father
> and he will give you another Paraclete—
> to be with you always:

the Spirit of truth,
whom the world cannot accept,
since it neither sees him nor recognizes him;
but you can recognize him
because he remains with you
and will be within you.
I will not leave you orphaned;
I will come back to you.
A little while now and the world will see me no more;
but you see me
as one who has life, and you will have life.
On that day you will know
that I am in my Father,
and you in me, and I in you.
He who obeys the commandments he has from me
is the man who loves me;
and he who loves me will be loved by my Father.
I too will love him
and reveal myself to him."

*. . . the Paraclete, the Holy Spirit . . . will instruct you in
everything . . .*

Judas (not Judas Iscariot) said to him, "Lord, why is it
that you will reveal yourself to us and not to the world?"
Jesus answered:

"Anyone who loves me
will be true to my word,
and my Father will love him;
we will come to him
and make our dwelling place with him.
He who does not love me does not keep my words.
Yet the word you hear is not mine;
it comes from the Father who sent me.

This much have I told you while I was still with you;
the Paraclete, the Holy Spirit
whom the Father will send in my name,
will instruct you in everything,
and remind you of all that I told you.
'Peace' is my farewell to you,
my peace is my gift to you;
I do not give it to you as the world gives peace.
Do not be distressed or fearful.
You have heard me say,
'I go away for a while, and I come back to you.'
If you truly loved me
you would rejoice to have me go to the Father,
for the Father is greater than I.
I tell you this now, before it takes place,
so that when it takes place you may believe.
I shall not go on speaking to you longer;
the Prince of this world is at hand.
He has no hold on me,
but the world must know that I love the Father
and do as the Father has commanded me."

When the Paraclete comes . . . he will bear witness on my behalf

Jn 15:26-27

"When the Paraclete comes,
the Spirit of truth who comes from the Father—
and whom I myself will send from the Father—
he will bear witness on my behalf.
You must bear witness as well,
for you have been with me from the beginning."

THE WORK OF THE HOLY SPIRIT

If I fail to go, the Paraclete will never come to you . . .

Jn 16:4-15

"I did not speak of this with you from the beginning
because I was with you.
Now that I go back to him who sent me,
not one of you asks me, 'Where are you going?'
Because I have had all this to say to you,
you are overcome with grief.
Yet I tell you the sober truth:
It is much better for you that I go.
If I fail to go,
the Paraclete will never come to you,
whereas if I go,
I will send him to you.
When he comes,
he will prove the world wrong
about sin,
about justice,
about condemnation.
About sin—
in that they refuse to believe in me;
about justice—
from the fact that I go to the Father
and you can see me no more;
about condemnation—
for the prince of this world has been condemned."

When the Spirit of truth comes . . . he will guide you to all truth

"I have much more to tell you,
but you cannot bear it now.
When he comes, however,
being the Spirit of truth
he will guide you to all truth.
He will not speak on his own,
but will speak only what he hears,
and will announce to you the things to come.
In doing this he will give glory to me,
because he will have received from me
what he will announce to you.
All that the Father has belongs to me.
That is why I said that what he will announce to you
he will have from me."

10. Jesus Appears to His Disciples

JESUS DIES ON THE CROSS

Father, into your hands I commend my spirit."

Lk 23:44-46

It was now around midday, and darkness came over the whole land until midafternoon with an eclipse of the sun. The curtain in the sanctuary was torn in two. Jesus uttered a loud cry and said,

"Father, into your hands I commend my spirit."

After he said this, he expired.

IN THE NAME OF THE THREE PERSONS

. . . baptize them in the name of the Father, the Son, and the Holy Spirit . . .

Mt 28:16-20

The eleven disciples made their way to Galilee, to the mountain to which Jesus had summoned them.

At the sight of him, those who had entertained

107

doubts fell down in homage. Jesus came forward and addressed them in these words:

"Full authority has been given to me
both in heaven and on earth;
go, therefore, and make disciples of all the nations.
Baptize them in the name
    'of the Father,
    and the Son,
    and the Holy Spirit.'
Teach them to carry out everything I have
    commanded you.
And know that I am with you always, until the
    end of the world!"

(parallel passage in Mark)
. . . they will speak entirely new languages . . .

Mk 16:15-18

Then he told them: "Go into the whole world and proclaim the good news to all creation. The man who believes in it and accepts baptism will be saved; the man who refuses to believe in it will be condemned. Signs like these will accompany those who have professed their faith: they will use my name to expel demons, they will speak entirely new languages, they will be able to handle serpents, they will be able to drink deadly poison without harm, and the sick upon whom they lay their hands will recover." Then, after speaking to them, the Lord Jesus was taken up into heaven and took his seat at God's right hand. The Eleven went forth and preached everywhere. The Lord continued to work with them throughout and confirm the message through the signs which accompanied them.

THE PROMISE OF THE FATHER

See, I send down upon you the promise of my Father

Lk 24:36-49

While they were still speaking about all this, he himself
stood in their midst [and said to them, "Peace to you"].
In their panic and fright they thought they were seeing
a ghost. He said to them, "Why are you disturbed?
Why do such ideas cross your mind? Look at my hands
and my feet; it is really I. Touch me, and see that
a ghost does not have flesh and bones as I do." As he
said this he showed them his hands and feet. They were
still incredulous for sheer joy and wonder, so he said
to them, "Have you anything here to eat?" They gave
him a piece of cooked fish, which he took and ate in
their presence. Then he said to them, "Recall those
words I spoke to you when I was still with you: everything written about me in the law of Moses and the
prophets and psalms had to be fulfilled." The he opened
their minds to the understanding of the Scriptures.

He said to them: "Thus it is written that the Messiah
must suffer and rise from the dead on the third day. 'In
his name, penance for the remission of sins is to be
preached to all the nations, beginning at Jerusalem. You
are witnesses of this. See, I send down upon you the
promise of my Father. Remain here in the city until
you are clothed with power from on high."

PEACE BE WITH YOU!

Receive the Holy Spirit

Jn 20:19-23

On the evening of that first day of the week, even though the disciples had locked the doors of the place where they were for fear of the Jews, Jesus came and stood before them. "Peace be with you," he said. When he had said this, he showed them his hands and his side. At the sight of the Lord the disciples rejoiced. "Peace be with you," he said again.

"As the Father has sent me, so I send you."
Then he breathed on them and said:

"Receive the Holy Spirit.
If you forgive men's sins,
they are forgiven them;
if you hold them bound,
they are held bound."

PART III

IN THE ACTS OF THE APOSTLES

1. The Promise of the Spirit

. . . within a few days you will be baptized with the Holy Spirit

Acts 1:1-11

In my first account, Theophilus, I dealt with all that Jesus did and taught until the day he was taken up to heaven, having first instructed the apostles he had chosen through the Holy Spirit. In the time after his suffering he showed them in many convincing ways that he was alive, appearing to them over the course of forty days and speaking to them about the reign of God. On one occasion when he met with them, he told them not to leave Jerusalem: "Wait, rather, for the fulfillment of my Father's promise, of which you have heard me speak. John baptized with water, but within a few days you will be baptized with the Holy Spirit."

While they were with him they asked, "Lord, are you going to restore the rule to Israel now?" His answer was: "The exact time it is not yours to know. The Father has reserved that to himself. You will receive power when the Holy Spirit comes down on you; then you are to be my witnesses in Jerusalem, throughout Judea and Samaria, yes, even to the end of the earth." No sooner had he said this than he was lifted up before their eyes in a cloud which took him from their sight.

MATTHIAS CHOSEN

. . . the saying in Scripture uttered long ago by the Holy Spirit . . . was destined to be fulfilled in Judas . . . "May another take his office"

Acts 1:15-26

At one point during those days, Peter stood up in the center of the brothers; there must have been a hundred and twenty gathered together. "Brothers," he said, "the saying in Scripture uttered long ago by the Holy Spirit through the mouth of David was destined to be fulfilled in Judas, the one who guided those that arrested Jesus. He was one of our number and he had been given a share in this ministry of ours . . . .

"It is written in the Book of Psalms, . . .

'May another take his office.'

It is entirely fitting, therefore, that one of those who was of our company while the Lord Jesus moved among us, from the baptism of John until the day he was taken up from us, should be named as witness with us to his resurrection." At that they nominated two, Joseph (called Barsabbas, also known as Justus) and Matthias. Then they prayed: "O Lord, you read the hearts of men. Make known to us which of these two you choose for this apostolic ministry, replacing Judas, who deserted the cause and went the way he was destined to go." They then drew lots between the two men. The choice fell to Matthias, who was added to the eleven apostles.

2. The Coming of the Spirit

All were filled with the Holy Spirit

Acts 2:1-13

When the day of Pentecost came it found them gathered
in one place. Suddenly from up in the sky there came
a noise like a strong, driving wind which was heard
all through the house where they were seated. Tongues
as of fire appeared, which parted and came to rest on
each of them. All were filled with the Holy Spirit. They
began to express themselves in foreign tongues and
make bold proclamation as the Spirit prompted them.

Staying in Jerusalem at the time were devout Jews
of every nation under heaven. These heard the sound,
and assembled in a large crowd. They were much con-
fused because each one heard these men speaking his
own language. The whole occurrence astonished them.
They asked in utter amazement, "Are not all of these
men who are speaking Galileans? How is it that each
of us hears them in his native tongue? We are Parthians,
Medes and Elamites. We live in Mesopotamia, Judea
and Cappadocia, Pontus, the province of Asia, Phrygia
and Pamphylia, Egypt, and the regions of Libya around
Cyrene. There are even visitors from Rome—all Jews,
or those who have come over to Judaism; Cretans and

Arabs too. Yet each of us hears them speaking in his own tongue about the marvels God has accomplished." They are dumbfounded, and could make nothing at all of what had happened.

"What does this mean?" they asked one another, while a few remarked with a sneer, "They have had too much new wine!"

PETER'S MESSAGE

. . . I will pour out a portion of my Spirit on all mankind

Acts 2:14-47

Peter stood up with the Eleven, raised his voice, and addressed them: "You who are Jews, indeed all of you staying in Jerusalem! Listen to what I have to say. You must realize that these men are not drunk, as you seem to think. It is only nine in the morning! No, it is what Joel the prophet spoke of:

'It shall come to pass in the last days, says God,
  that I will pour out a portion of my spirit on
    all mankind:
Your sons and daughters shall prophesy,
  your young men shall see visions
  and your old men shall dream dreams.
Yes, even on my servants and handmaids
  I will pour out a portion of my spirit in
    those days,
  and they shall prophesy.
I will work wonders in the heavens above
  and signs on the earth below:
  blood, fire, and a cloud of smoke.

116

The sun shall be turned to darkness and the
    moon to blood
    before the coming of that great and glorious
      day of the Lord.
Then shall everyone be saved who calls on the
    name of the Lord."

*. . . Jesus first received the promised Holy Spirit from
the Father, then poured his Spirit out on us*

"Men of Israel, listen to me! Jesus the Nazorean was
a man whom God sent to you with miracles, wonders,
and signs as his credentials. These God worked through
him in your midst, as you well know. He was delivered
up by the set purpose and plan of God; you even
made use of pagans to crucify and kill him. God freed
him from death's bitter pangs, however, and raised him
up again, for it was impossible that death should keep
its hold on him. David says of him:

'I have set the Lord ever before me,
    with him at my right hand I shall not be
      disturbed.
My heart has been glad and my tongue has
    rejoiced,
    my body will live on in hope,
for you will not abandon my soul to the nether
    world,
    nor will you suffer your faithful one to
      undergo corruption.
You have shown me the paths of life;
    you will fill me with joy in your presence.'

"Brothers, I can speak confidently to you about our
father David. He died and was buried, and his grave is

in our midst to this day. He was a prophet and knew that God had sworn to him that one of his descendants would sit upon his throne. He said that he was not abandoned to the nether world, nor did his body undergo corruption, thus proclaiming beforehand the resurrection of the Messiah. This is the Jesus God has raised up, and we are his witnesses. Exalted at God's right hand, he first received the promised Holy Spirit from the Father, then poured this Spirit out on us. This is what you now see and hear. David did not go up to heaven, yet David says,

> 'The Lord said to my Lord,
>> Sit at my right hand
>> until I make your enemies your footstool.'

Therefore let the whole house of Israel know beyond any doubt that God has made both Lord and Messiah this Jesus whom you crucified."

. . . then you will receive the gift of the Holy Spirit. It was to you and your children that the promise was made . . .

When they heard this, they were deeply shaken. They asked Peter and the other apostles, "What are we to do, brothers?" Peter answered: "You must reform and be baptized, each one of you, in the name of Jesus Christ, that your sins may be forgiven; then you will receive the gift of the Holy Spirit. It was to you and your children that the promise was made, and to all those still far off whom the Lord our God calls."

In support of his testimony he used many other arguments, and kept urging, "Save yourselves from this generation which has gone astray." Those who accepted his message were baptized; some three thousand were added that day.

They devoted themselves to the apostles' instruction and the communal life, to the breaking of bread and the prayers. A reverent fear overtook them all, for many wonders and signs were performed by the apostles. Those who believed shared all things in common; they would sell their property and goods, dividing everything on the basis of each one's need. They went to the temple area together every day, while in their homes they broke bread. With exultant and sincere hearts they took their meals in common, praising God and winning the approval of all the people. Day by day the Lord added to their number those who were being saved.

PETER AND JOHN BEFORE THE SANHEDRIN

Then Peter, filled with the Holy Spirit, spoke up . . .

Acts 4:1-22

While Peter and John were still addressing the crowd, the priests, the captain of the temple guard, and the Sadducees came up to them, angry because they were teaching the people and proclaiming the resurrection of the dead in the person of Jesus. It was evening by now, so they arrested them and put them in jail for the night. Despite this, many of those who had heard the speech believed; the number of the men came to about five thousand.

When the leaders, the elders, and the scribes assembled the next day in Jerusalem, Annas the high priest, Caiaphas, John, Alexander, and all who were of the high-priestly class were there. They brought Peter and John before them and began the interrogation in this fashion: "By what power or in whose name have men of your stripe done this?"

Then Peter, filled with the Holy Spirit, spoke up: "Leaders of the people! Elders! If we must answer today for a good deed done to a cripple and explain how he was restored to health, then you and all the people of Israel must realize that it was done in the name of Jesus Christ the Nazorean whom you crucified and whom God raised from the dead. In the power of that name this man stands before you perfectly sound. This Jesus is 'the stone rejected by you the builders which has become the cornerstone.' There is no salvation in anyone else, for there is no other name in the whole world given to men by which we are to be saved."

Observing the self-assurance of Peter and John, and realizing that the speakers were uneducated men of no standing, the questioners were amazed. Then they recognized these men as having been with Jesus. When they saw the man who had been cured standing there with them, they could think of nothing to say, so they ordered them out of the court while they held a consultation. "What shall we do with these men? Everyone who lives in Jerusalem knows what a remarkable show of power took place through them. We cannot deny it. To stop this from spreading further among the people we must give them a stern warning never to mention that man's name to anyone again." So they called them back and made it clear that under no circumstances were they to speak the name of Jesus or teach about

120

him. Peter and John answered, "Judge for yourselves whether it is right in God's sight for us to obey you rather than God. Surely we cannot help speaking of what we have heard and seen." At that point they were dismissed with further warnings. The court could find no way to punish them because of the people, all of whom were praising God for what had happened. The fact was, the man thus miraculously cured was more than forty years of age.

THE BELIEVERS PRAY

The place where they were gathered shook as they prayed. They were filled with the Holy Spirit . . .

Acts 4:23-35

After being released, the two went back to their own people and told them what the priests and elders had said. All raised their voices in prayer to God on hearing the story: "Sovereign Lord, who made heaven and earth and sea and all that is in them, you have said by the Holy Spirit through the lips of our father David your servant:

'Why did the Gentiles rage
the peoples conspire in folly?
The kings of the earth were aligned,
the princes gathered together
against the Lord and against his anointed.'

Indeed, they gathered in this very city against your holy Servant, Jesus, whom you anointed—Herod and Pontius Pilate in league with the Gentiles and the

121

peoples of Israel. They have brought about the very
things which in your powerful providence you planned
long ago. But now, O Lord, look at the threats they are
leveling against us. Grant to your servants, even as they
speak your words, complete assurance by stretching
forth your hand in cures and signs and wonders to be
worked in the name of Jesus, your holy Servant."

The place where they were gathered shook as they
prayed. They were filled with the Holy Spirit and continued to speak God's word with confidence. The community of believers were of one heart and one mind.
None of them ever claimed anything as his own; rather,
everything was held in common. With power the
apostles bore witness to the resurrection of the Lord
Jesus, and great respect was paid to them all; nor was
there anyone needy among them, for all who owned
property or houses sold them and donated the proceeds.
They used to lay them at the feet of the apostles to be
distributed to everyone according to his need.

ANANIAS AND SAPPHIRA

*. . . why have you let Satan fill your heart so as to make
you lie to the Holy Spirit? . . .*

Acts 5:1-15

Another man named Ananias and his wife Sapphira likewise sold a piece of property. With the connivance of
his wife he put aside a part of the proceeds for himself;
the rest he took and laid at the feet of the apostles.
Peter exclaimed: "Ananias, why have you let Satan fill
your heart so as to make you lie to the Holy Spirit and
keep for yourself some of the proceeds from that field?

122

Was it not yours so long as it remained unsold? Even when you sold it, was not the money still yours? How could you ever concoct such a scheme? You have lied not to men but to God!" At the sound of these words, Ananias fell dead. Great fear came upon all who later heard of it. Some of the young men came forward, wrapped up the body, and carried it out for burial. Three hours later Ananias' wife came in, unaware of what had happened. Peter said to her, "Tell me, did you sell that piece of property for such and such an amount?" She answered, "Yes, that was the sum." Peter replied, "How could you two scheme to put the Spirit of the Lord to the test? The footsteps of the men who have just buried your husband can be heard at the door. They stand ready to carry you out too." At that, she fell dead at his feet. The young men came in, found her dead, and carried her out for burial beside her husband. Great fear came on the whole church and on all who heard of it.

Through the hands of the apostles, many signs and wonders occurred among the people. By mutual agreement they used to meet in Solomon's Portico. No one else dared to join them, despite the fact that the people held them in great esteem. Nevertheless more and more believers, men and women in great numbers, were continually added to the Lord. The people carried the sick into the streets and laid them on cots and mattresses, so that when Peter passed by at least his shadow might fall on one or another of them. Crowds from the towns around Jerusalem would gather, too, bringing their sick and those who were troubled by unclean spirits, all of whom were cured.

SECOND TIME BEFORE THE SANHEDRIN

We testify to this. So too does the Holy Spirit . . .

Acts 5:27-42

When they had led them in and made them stand before the Sanhedrin, the high priest began the interrogation in this way: "We gave you strict orders not to teach about that name, yet you have filled Jerusalem with your teaching and are determined to make us responsible for that man's blood." To this, Peter and the apostles replied: "Better for us to obey God than men! The God of our fathers has raised up Jesus whom you put to death, hanging him on a tree. He whom God has exalted at his right hand as ruler and savior is to bring repentance to Israel and forgiveness of sins. We testify to this. So too does the Holy Spirit, whom God has given to those that obey him."

When the Sanhedrin heard this, they were stung to fury and wanted to kill them. Then a member of the Sanhedrin stood up, a Pharisee named Gamaliel, a teacher of the law highly regarded by all the people. He had the accused ordered out of court for a few minutes, and then said to the assembly, "Fellow Israelites, think twice about what you are going to do with these men. Not long ago a certain Theudas came on the scene and tried to pass himself off as someone of importance. About four hundred men joined him. However he was killed, and all those who had been so easily convinced by him were disbanded. In the end it came to nothing. Next came Judas the Galilean at the time of the census. He too built up quite a following, but likewise died, and all his followers were dispersed. The present case is similar. My advice is that you have nothing to do with these men. Let them alone. If their purpose or activity is human in its origins, it will destroy itself. If, on the other hand, it comes from God, you will not be able to destroy them without fighting God himself."

This speech persuaded them. In spite of it, however, the Sanhedrin called in the apostles and had them whipped. They ordered them not to speak again about the name of Jesus, and afterward dismissed them. The apostles for their part left the Sanhedrin full of joy that they had been judged worthy of ill treatment for the sake of the Name. Day after day, both in the temple and at home, they never stopped teaching and proclaiming the good news of Jesus the Messiah.

3. Stephen

. . . they selected Stephen, a man filled with faith and the Holy Spirit

Acts 6:1-7

In those days, as the number of disciples grew, the ones who spoke Greek complained that their widows were being neglected in the daily distribution of food, as compared with the widows of those who spoke Hebrew. The Twelve assembled the community of the disciples and said, "It is not right for us to neglect the word of God in order to wait on tables. Look around among your own number, brothers, for seven men acknowledged to be deeply spiritual and prudent, and we shall appoint them to this task. This will permit us to consecrate on prayer and the ministry of the word." The proposal was unanimously accepted by the community. Following this they selected Stephen, a man filled with faith and the Holy Spirit; Philip, Prochorus, Nicanor, Timon, Parmenas, and Nicolaus of Antioch, who had been a convert to Judaism. They presented these men to the apostles, who first prayed over them and then imposed hands on them.

The word of God continued to spread, while at the same time the number of the disciples in Jerusalem enormously increased. There were many priests among those who embraced the faith.

STEPHEN ACCUSED

. . . they proved no match for the wisdom and spirit with which Stephen spoke

Acts 6:8-15

The Stephen already spoken of was a man filled with grace and power, who worked great wonders and signs among the people. Certain members of the so-called "Synagogue of Roman Freedmen" (that is, the Jews from Cyrene, Alexandria, Cilicia and Asia) would undertake to engage Stephen in debate, but they proved no match for the wisdom and spirit with which he spoke.* They persuaded some men to make the charge that they had heard him speaking blasphemies against Moses and God, and in this way they incited the people, the elders, and the scribes. All together they confronted him, seized him, and led him off to the Sanhedrin. There they brought in false witnesses, who said: "This man never stops making statements against the holy place and the law. We have heard him claim that Jesus the Nazorean will destroy this place and change the customs which Moses handed down to us." The members of the Sanhedrin who sat there stared at him intently. Throughout, Stephen's face seemed like that of an angel.

---

*RSV reads: But they could not withstand the wisdom and the Spirit with which he spoke.

STEPHEN'S ANSWER

. . . you are always opposing the Holy Spirit just as your fathers did before you

Acts 7:1-2, 51-53

The high priest asked whether the charges were true. To this Stephen replied: "My brothers! Fathers! Listen to me."

• • • •

Conclusion of long speech
"You stiff-necked people, uncircumcised in heart and ears, you are always opposing the Holy Spirit just as your fathers did before you. Was there ever any prophet whom your fathers did not persecute? In their day, they put to death those who foretold the coming of the Just One; now you in your turn have become his betrayers and murderers. You who received the law through the ministry of angels have not observed it."

STEPHEN MARTYRED

Stephen, full of the Spirit . . . saw the glory of God . . .

Acts 7:54-60; 8:1-3

Those who listened to his words were stung to the heart; they ground their teeth in anger at him. Stephen meanwhile, filled with the Holy Spirit, looked to the sky above and saw the glory of God, and Jesus standing at God's right hand. "Look" he exclaimed, "I see an opening in the sky, and the Son of Man standing at God's right hand." The onlookers were shouting aloud, holding their hands over their ears as they did so. Then they rushed at him as one man, dragged him out of the city, and began to stone him. The witnesses meanwhile were piling their cloaks at the feet of a young man named Saul. As Stephen was being stoned he could be heard praying, "Lord Jesus, receive my spirit." He fell to his knees and cried out in a loud voice, "Lord, do not hold this sin against them." And with that he died.

Saul, for his part, concurred in the act of killing. That day saw the beginning of a great persecution of the church in Jerusalem. All except the apostles scattered throughout the countryside of Judea and Samaria. Devout men buried Stephen, bewailing him loudly as they did so. After that, Saul began to harass the church. He entered house after house, dragged men and women out, and threw them into jail.

4. Samaritans Receive the Spirit

*. . . the pair imposed hands on them and they received
the Holy Spirit*

Acts 8:4-25

The members of the church who had been dispersed
went about preaching the word. Philip, for example,
went down to the town of Samaria and there proclaimed
the Messiah. Without exception, the crowds that heard
Philip and saw the miracles he performed attended
closely to what he had to say. There were many who
came out shrieking loudly. Many others were paralytics
or cripples, and these were cured. The rejoicing in that
town rose to fever pitch.

A certain man named Simon had been practicing
magic in the town and holding the Samaritans spell-
bound. He passed himself off as someone of great
importance. People from every rank of society were
paying attention to him. "He is the power of the great
God," they said. Those who followed him had been under
the spell of his magic over a long period; but once they
began to believe in the good news that Philip preached
about the kingdom of God and the name of Jesus Christ,
men and women alike accepted baptism. Even Simon
believed. He was baptized like the rest and became a

devoted follower of Philip. He watched the signs and the great miracles as they occurred, and was quite carried away.

When the apostles in Jerusalem heard that Samaria had accepted the word of God, they sent Peter and John to them. The two went down to these people and prayed that they might receive the Holy Spirit. It had not as yet come down upon any of them since they had only been baptized in the name of the Lord Jesus. The pair upon arriving imposed hands on them and they received the Holy Spirit. Simon observed that it was through the laying on of hands that the apostles conferred the Spirit and he made them an offer of money with the request, "Give me that power too, so that if I place my hands on anyone he will receive the Holy Spirit."

Peter said in answer: "May you and your money rot—thinking that God's gift can be bought! You can have no portion or lot in this affair. Your heart is not steadfastly set on God. Reform your evil ways. Pray that the Lord may pardon you for thinking the way you have. I see you poisoned with gall and caught in the grip of sin." Simon responded, "I need the prayers of all of you to the Lord, so that what you have just said may never happen to me."

PHILIP AND THE ETHIOPIAN

The Spirit said to Philip, "Go and catch up with that carriage."

Acts 8:26-40

An angel of the Lord then addressed himself to Philip:
"Head south toward the road which goes from Jerusalem
to Gaza, the desert route." Philip began the journey.
It happened that an Ethiopian eunuch, a court official in
charge of the entire treasury of Candace (a name meaning queen) of the Ethiopians, had come on a pilgrimage
to Jerusalem and was returning home. He was sitting
in his carriage reading the prophet Isaiah. The Spirit
said to Philip, "Go and catch up with that carriage."
Philip ran ahead and heard the man reading Isaiah. He
said to him, "Do you really grasp what you are reading?" "How can I," the man replied, "unless someone
explains it to me?" With that, he invited Philip to get in
and sit down beside him. This was the passage of Scripture he was reading:

> "Like a sheep he was led to the slaughter,
>> like a lamb before its shearer he was silent
>> and opened not his mouth.
> In his humiliation he was deprived of justice.
>> Who will ever speak of his posterity,
>> for he is deprived of his life on earth?"

The eunuch said to Philip, "Tell me, if you will,
of whom the prophet says this—himself or someone
else?" Philip launched out with this Scripture passage as
his starting point, telling him the good news of Jesus.
As they moved along the road they came to some

water, and the eunuch said, "Look, there is some water right there. What is to keep me from being baptized?" He ordered the carriage stopped, and Philip went down into the water with the eunuch and baptized him. When they came out of the water, the Spirit of the Lord snatched Philip away and the eunuch saw him no more. Nevertheless the man went on his way rejoicing. Philip found himself at Azotus next, and he went about announcing the good news in all the towns until he reached Caesarea.

5. Saul Filled with the Holy Spirit

SAUL CONVERTED

*I have been sent by the Lord Jesus . . . to help you
recover your sight and be filled with the Holy Spirit*

Acts 9:1-19

Saul, still breathing murderous threats against the Lord's
disciples, went to the high priest and asked him for
letters to the synagogues in Damascus which would em-
power him to arrest and bring to Jerusalem anyone he
might find, man or woman, living according to the new
way. As he traveled along and was approaching Damascus, a light from the sky suddenly flashed about him.
He fell to the ground and at the same time heard a
voice saying, "Saul, Saul, why do you persecute me?"
"Who are you, sir?" he asked. The voice answered, "I
am Jesus, the one you are persecuting. Get up and
go into the city, where you will be told what to do." The
men who were traveling with him stood there speechless.
They had heard the voice but could see no one. Saul got
up from the ground unable to see, even though his eyes
were open. They had to take him by the hand and
lead him into Damascus. For three days he continued
blind, during which time he neither ate nor drank.

There was a disciple in Damascus named Ananias to

whom the Lord had appeared in a vision. "Ananias!" he said. "Here I am, Lord," came the answer. The Lord said to him, "Go at once to Straight Street, and at the house of Judas ask for a certain Saul of Tarsus. He is there praying." (Saul saw in a vision a man named Ananias coming to him and placing his hands on him so that he might recover his sight.) But Ananias protested: "Lord, I have heard from many sources about this man and all the harm he has done to your holy people in Jerusalem. He is here now with authorization from the chief priests to arrest any who invoke your name." The Lord said to him: "You must go! This man is the instrument I have chosen to bring my name to the Gentiles and their kings and to the people of Israel. I myself shall indicate to him how much he will have to suffer for my name." With that Ananias left. When he entered the house he laid his hands on Saul and said, "Saul, my brother, I have been sent by the Lord Jesus who appeared to you on the way here, to help you recover your sight and be filled with the Holy Spirit." Immediately something like scales fell from his eyes and he regained his sight. He got up and was baptized, and his strength returned to him after he had taken food.

SAUL BACK IN JERUSALEM

The Church was at peace . . . it enjoyed the increased consolation of the Holy Spirit

Acts 9:26-31

When he arrived back in Jerusalem he tried to join the disciples there; but it turned out that they were all afraid of him. They even refused to believe that he was a disciple. Then Barnabas took him in charge and

135

introduced him to the apostles. He explained to them how on his journey Saul had seen the Lord, who had conversed with him, and how Saul had been speaking out fearlessly in the name of Jesus at Damascus. Saul stayed on with them, moving freely about Jerusalem and expressing himself quite openly in the name of the Lord. He even addressed the Greek-speaking Jews and debated with them. They for their part responded by trying to kill him. When the brothers learned of this, some of them took him down to Caesarea and sent him off to Tarsus.

Meanwhile throughout all Judea, Galilee, and Samaria the church was at peace. It was being built up and was making steady progress in the fear of the Lord; at the same time it enjoyed the increased consolation of the Holy Spirit.

6. The Gentiles Receive the Holy Spirit

PETER AND CORNELIUS

The Holy Spirit descended on all who were listening to Peter's message

Acts 10:1-48

The Vision of Cornelius
Now in Caesarea there was a centurion named Cornelius, of the Roman cohort Italica, who was religious and God-fearing. The same was true of his whole household. He was in the habit of giving generously to the people and he constantly prayed to God. One afternoon at about three he had a vision in which he clearly saw a messenger of God coming toward him and calling, "Cornelius!" He stared at the sight and said in fear, "What is it, sir?" The answer came: "Your prayers and your generosity have risen in God's sight, and because of them he has remembered you. Send some men to Joppa and summon a certain Simon, known as Peter. He is a guest of Simon the leather-tanner whose house stands by the sea." When the messenger who spoke these words had disappeared, he called two servants and a devout soldier from among those whom he could trust. He explained everything to them and dispatched them to Joppa.

Peter's Vision

About noontime the next day, as the men were
traveling along and approaching the city, Peter went up
to the roof terrace to pray. He became hungry and asked
for some food, and while it was being prepared he fell
into a trance. He saw the sky open and an object come
down that looked like a big canvas. It was lowered to
the ground by its four corners. Inside it were all the
earth's four-legged creatures and reptiles and birds of
the sky. A voice said to him: "Get up, Peter! Slaughter,
then eat." He answered: "Sir, it is unthinkable! I have
never eaten anything unclean or impure in my life." The
voice was heard a second time: "What God has purified
you are not to call unclean." This happened three times;
then the object was snatched up into the sky. While Peter
was trying to make out the meaning of the vision he had
had, the men sent by Cornelius arrived at the gate
asking for the house of Simon. They called out to
inquire whether Simon Peter was a guest there. Peter was
still pondering the vision when the Spirit said to him:
"There are two men in search of you. Go downstairs and
set out with them unhesitatingly, for it is I who sent
them." Peter went down to the men and said, "I am the
man you are looking for. What brought you here?"
They answered: "The centurion Cornelius, who is an
upright and God-fearing man, well thought of in the
whole Jewish community, has been instructed by a holy
messenger to summon you to his house. There he is to
hear what you have to say." With that, Peter invited
them in and treated them as guests.

Peter in Caesarea

The next day he went off with them, accompanied by
some of the brothers from Joppa. The following day,
he arrived in Caesarea. Cornelius, who was expecting

them, had called in his relatives and close friends. As Peter entered, Cornelius went to meet him, dropped to his knees before him and bowed low. Peter said as he helped him to his feet, "Get up! I am only a man myself." Peter then went in, talking with him all the while. He found many people assembled there, and he began speaking to them thus: "You must know that it is not proper for a Jew to associate with a Gentile or to have dealings with him. But God has made it clear to me that no one should call any man unclean or impure. That is why I have come in response to your summons without raising any objection. I should, of course, like to know why you summoned me." Cornelius replied: "Just three days ago at this very hour, namely three o'clock, I was praying at home when a man in dazzling robes stood before me. 'Cornelius,' he said, 'your prayer has been heard and your generosity remembered in God's presence. Send someone to Joppa to invite Simon known as Peter to come here. He is a guest in the house of Simon the leather-tanner, by the sea.' I sent for you immediately, and you have been kind enough to come. All of us stand before God at this moment to hear whatever directives the Lord has given you."

Peter's Discourse
Peter proceeded to address them in these words: "I begin to see how true it is that God shows no partiality. Rather, the man of any nation who fears God and acts uprightly is acceptable to him. This is the message he has sent to the sons of Israel, the good news of peace proclaimed through Jesus Christ who is Lord of all. I take it you know what has been reported all over Judea about Jesus of Nazareth, beginning in Galilee with the baptism John preached; of the way God anointed him with the Holy Spirit and power. He went about doing

139

good works and healing all who were in the grip of the devil, and God was with him. We are witnesses to all that he did in the land of the Jews and in Jerusalem. They killed him, finally, hanging him on a tree, only to have God raise him up on the third day and grant that he be seen, not by all, but only by such witnesses as had been chosen beforehand by God—by us who ate and drank with him after he rose from the dead. He commissioned us to preach to the people and to bear witness that he is the one set apart by God as judge of the living and the dead. To him all the prophets testify, saying that everyone who believes in him has forgiveness of sins through his name."

Baptism of Cornelius

Peter had not finished these words when the Holy Spirit descended upon all who were listening to Peter's message. The circumcised believers who had accompanied Peter were surprised that the gift of the Holy Spirit should have been poured out on the Gentiles also, whom they could hear speaking in tongues and glorifying God. Peter put the question at that point: "What can stop these people who have received the Holy Spirit, even as we have, from being baptized with water?" So he gave orders that they be baptized in the name of Jesus Christ. After this was done, they asked him to stay with them for a few days.

THE CALL OF THE GENTILES EXPLAINED

As I began to address them, the Holy Spirit came upon them, just as he had upon us at the beginning

Acts 11:1-18

All through Judea the apostles and the brothers heard that Gentiles, too, had accepted the word of God. As a result, when Peter went up to Jerusalem some among the circumcised took issue with him, saying, "You entered the house of uncircumcised men and ate with them." Peter then explained the whole affair to them step by step from the beginning. "I was at prayer in the city of Joppa when, in a trance, I saw a vision. . . . (see p. 138)

"Immediately after that, the three men who had been sent to me from Caesarea came to the house where we were staying. The Spirit instructed me to accompany them without hesitation. These six brothers came along with me, and we entered the man's house. He informed us that he had seen an angel standing in his house and that the angel had said: 'Send someone to Joppa and fetch Simon, known also as Peter. In the light of what he will tell you, you shall be saved, and all your household.' As I began to address them the Holy Spirit came upon them, just as it had upon us at the beginning. Then I remembered what the Lord had said: 'John baptized with water but you will be baptized with the Holy Spirit.' If God was giving them the same gift he gave us when we first believed in the Lord Jesus Christ, who was I to interfere with him?" When they heard this they stopped objecting, and instead began to glorify God in these words: "If this be so, then God has granted lifegiving repentance even to the Gentiles."

141

THE CHURCH AT ANTIOCH

Barnabas . . . a good man filled with the Holy Spirit and faith . . .

Acts 11:19-30

Those in the community who had been dispersed by the persecution that arose because of Stephen went as far as Phoenicia, Cyprus and Antioch, making the message known to none but Jews. However, some men of Cyprus and Cyrene among them who had come to Antioch began to talk even to the Greeks, announcing the good news of the Lord Jesus to them. The hand of the Lord was with them and a great number of them believed and were converted to the Lord. News of this eventually reached the ears of the church in Jerusalem, resulting in Barnabas' being sent to Antioch.

On his arrival he rejoiced to see the evidence of God's favor. He encouraged them all to remain firm in their commitment to the Lord, since he himself was a good man filled with the Holy Spirit and faith. Thereby large numbers were added to the Lord. Then Barnabas went off to Tarsus to look for Saul; once he had found him, he brought him back to Antioch. For a whole year they met with the church and instructed great numbers. It was in Antioch that the disciples were called Christians for the first time.

THE MISSION OF BARNABAS AND SAUL

*. . . the Holy Spirit spoke to them: "Set aside Barnabas
and Saul for me . . ."*

Acts 13:1-12

There were in the church at Antioch certain prophets
and teachers: Barnabas, Symeon known as Niger, Lucius
of Cyrene, Manaen (who had been brought up with
Herod the tetrarch), and Saul. On one occasion, while
they were engaged in the liturgy of the Lord and were
fasting, the Holy Spirit spoke to them: "Set apart
Barnabas and Saul for me to do the work for which I
have called them." Then, after they had fasted and
prayed, they imposed hands on them and sent them off.

Saul . . . filled with the Holy Spirit, stared at him . . .

These two, sent forth by the Holy Spirit, went down to
the port of Seleucia and set sail from there for Cyprus.
On their arrival in Salamis they proclaimed the word of
God in the Jewish synagogues, John accompanying them
as an assistant. They traveled over the whole island as
far as Paphos, where they came across a Jewish magician
named Bar-Jesus who posed as a prophet. He was
attached to the court of the proconsular governor Sergius
Paulus, a man of intelligence who had summoned
Barnabas and Saul and was anxious to hear the word of
God. But Elymas—"the magician," for that is what his
name means—opposed them and sought to turn the
governor away from the faith. Saul (also known as
Paul) was filled with the Holy Spirit; he stared at him
and exclaimed: "You are an impostor and a thorough-
going fraud, you son of Satan and enemy of all that is

right! Will you never stop trying to make crooked the straight paths of the Lord? The Lord's hand is upon you even now! For a time you shall be blind, unable so much as to see the sun." At once a misty darkness came over him, and he groped about for someone to lead him by the hand. When the governor saw what had happened, he believed, so impressed was he by the teaching about the Lord.

The disciples could not but be filled with joy and the Holy Spirit

Acts 13:44-52

The following sabbath, almost the entire city gathered to hear the word of God. When the Jews saw the crowds, they became very jealous and countered with violent abuse whatever Paul said. Paul and Barnabas spoke out fearlessly, nonetheless: "The word of God has to be declared to you first of all; but since you reject it and thus convict yourselves as unworthy of everlasting life, we now turn to the Gentiles. For thus were we instructed by the Lord: 'I have made you a light to the nations, a means of salvation to the ends of the earth.'" The Gentiles were delighted when they heard this and responded to the word of the Lord with praise. All who were destined for life everlasting believed in it. Thus the word of the Lord was carried throughout that area.

But some of the Jews stirred up their influential women sympathizers and the leading men of the town, and in that way got a persecution started against Paul and Barnabas. The Jews finally expelled them from their territory. So the two shook the dust from their feet in protest and went on to Iconium. The disciples could not but be filled with joy and the Holy Spirit.

THE COUNCIL AT JERUSALEM

*God . . . showed his approval by granting the Holy
Spirit to them (the Gentiles) just as he did to us*

Acts 15:1-12

Some men came down to Antioch from Judea and began
to teach the brothers: "Unless you are circumcised according to Mosaic practice, you cannot be saved." This
created dissension and much controversy between them
and Paul and Barnabas, Finally it was decided that Paul,
Barnabas, and some others should go up to see the
apostles and presbyters in Jerusalem about this question.
    The church saw them off and they made their way
through Phoenicia and Samaria, telling everyone about
the conversion of the Gentiles as they went. Their story
caused great joy among the brothers. When they arrived
in Jerusalem they were welcomed by that church, as well
as by the apostles and the presbyters, to whom they
reported all that God had helped them accomplish. Some
of the converted Pharisees then got up and demanded
that such Gentiles be circumcised and told to keep the
Mosaic law.
    The apostles and the presbyters accordingly convened
to look into the matter. After much discussion, Peter
took the floor and said to them: "Brothers, you know
well enough that from the early days God selected me
from your number to be the one from whose lips the
Gentiles would hear the message of the gospel and
believe. God, who reads the hearts of men, showed his
approval by granting the Holy Spirit to them just as he
did to us. He made no distinction between them and us,
but purified their hearts by means of faith also. Why,
then, do you put God to the test by trying to place on the

shoulders of these converts a yoke which neither we nor our fathers were able to bear? Our belief is rather that we are saved by the favor of the Lord Jesus and so are they." At that the whole assembly fell silent. They listened to Barnabas and Paul as the two described all the signs and wonders God had worked among the Gentiles through them.

It is the decision of the Holy Spirit . . .

Acts 15:22-29

It was resolved by the apostles and the presbyters, in agreement with the whole Jerusalem church, that representatives be chosen from among their number and sent to Antioch along with Paul and Barnabas. Those chosen were leading men of the community, Judas, known as Barsabbas, and Silas. They were to deliver this letter:
"The apostles and the presbyters, your brothers, send greetings to the brothers of Gentile origin in Antioch, Syria, and Cilicia. We have heard that some of our number without any instructions from us have upset you with their discussions and disturbed your peace of mind. Therefore we have unanimously resolved to choose representatives and send them to you, along with our beloved Barnabas and Paul, who have dedicated themselves to the cause of our Lord Jesus Christ. Those whom we are sending you are Judas and Silas, who will convey this message by word of mouth: 'It is the decision of the Holy Spirit, and ours too, not to lay on you any burden beyond that which is strictly necessary, namely, to abstain from meat sacrificed to idols, from blood, from the meat of strangled animals, and from illicit sexual union. You will be well advised to avoid these things. Farewell.' "

7. Paul's Mission

GUIDED BY THE SPIRIT

... the Spirit of Jesus did not allow them to go

Acts 16:6-10

They next traveled through Phrygia and Galatian territory because they had been prevented by the Holy Spirit from preaching the message in the province of Asia. When they came to Mysia they tried to go on into Bithynia, but again the Spirit of Jesus would not allow them. Crossing through Mysia instead, they came down to Troas. There one night Paul had a vision. A man of Macedonia stood before him and invited him, "Come over to Macedonia and help us."

After this vision, we immediately made efforts to get across to Macedonia, concluding that God had summoned us to proclaim the good news there.

PAUL AT EPHESUS

We have not so much as heard that there is a
Holy Spirit

Acts 19:1-10

While Apollos was in Corinth, Paul passed through the
interior of the country and came to Ephesus. There he
found some disciples to whom he put the question, "Did
you receive the Holy Spirit when you became believers?"
They answered, "We have not so much as heard that
there is a Holy Spirit." "Well, how were you baptized?"
he persisted. They replied, "With the baptism of John."
Paul then explained, "John's baptism was a baptism of
repentance. He used to tell the people about the one who
would come after him in whom they were to believe—
that is, Jesus." When they heard this, they were baptized
in the name of the Lord Jesus. As Paul laid his hands on
them, the Holy Spirit came down on them and they
began to speak in tongues and to utter prophecies. There
were in the company about twelve men in all.

Paul entered the synagogue, and over a period of
three months debated fearlessly, with persuasive
arguments, about the kingdom of God. When some in
their obstinacy would not believe, but chose to speak ill
of the new way in the presence of the assembly, Paul
simply left them. He took his disciples with him, and
after that held his discussions from day to day in the
lecture hall of Tyrannus. This continued for two years,
with the result that all the inhabitants of the province of
Asia, Jews and Greeks alike, heard the word of the
Lord. Meanwhile God worked extraordinary miracles at
the hands of Paul. When handkerchiefs or cloths which
had touched his skin were applied to the sick, their
diseases were cured and evil spirits departed from them.

PAUL'S FAREWELL SPEECH TO THE PRESBYTERS

I am on my way to Jerusalem, compelled by the Spirit ...

Acts 20:16-38

Paul had decided to sail past Ephesus so as not to lose time in Asia, for he was eager to get to Jerusalem by the feast of Pentecost if at all possible.

Paul sent word from Miletus to Ephesus, summoning the presbyters of that church. When they came to him he delivered this address: "You know how I lived among you from the first day I set foot in the province of Asia —how I served the Lord in humility through the sorrows and trials that came my way from the plottings of certain Jews. Never did I shrink from telling you what was for your own good, or from teaching you in public or in private. With Jews and Greeks alike I insisted solemnly on repentance before God and on faith in our Lord Jesus. But now, as you see, I am on my way to Jerusalem, compelled by the Spirit and not knowing what will happen to me there—except that the Holy Spirit has been warning me from city to city that chains and hardships await me. I put no value on my life if only I can finish my race and complete the service to which I have been assigned by the Lord Jesus, bearing witness to the gospel of God's grace. I know as I speak these words that none of you among whom I went about preaching the kingdom will ever see my face again. Therefore I solemnly declare this day that I take the blame for no man's conscience, for I have never shrunk from announcing to you God's design in its entirety."

. . . the flock the Holy Spirit has given you . . .

"Keep watch over yourselves, and over the whole flock the Holy Spirit has given you to guard. Shepherd the church of God, which he has acquired at the price of his own blood. I know that when I am gone, savage wolves will come among you who will not spare the flock. From your own number, men will present themselves distorting the truth and leading astray any who follow them. Be on guard, therefore. Do not forget that for three years, night and day, I never ceased warning you individually even to the point of tears. I commend you now to the Lord, and to that gracious word of his which can enlarge you, and give you a share among all who are consecrated to him. Never did I set my heart on anyone's silver or gold or envy the way he dressed. You yourselves know that these hands of mine have served both my needs and those of my companions. I have always pointed out to you that it is by such hard work that you must help the weak. You need to recall the words of the Lord Jesus himself, who said, 'There is more happiness in giving than receiving.' "

After this discourse, Paul knelt down with them all and prayed. They began to weep without restraint, throwing their arms around him and kissing him, for they were deeply distressed to hear that they would never see his face again. Then they escorted him to the ship.

PAUL ON THE WAY TO JERUSALEM

Under the Spirit's prompting, they tried to tell Paul that he should not go up to Jerusalem

Acts 21:1-14

When we had finally taken leave of them, we put out to sea and sailed straight to Cos. On the following day we came to Rhodes and went on from there to Patara. When

150

we found a ship bound for Phoenicia, we boarded it and sailed off. We caught sight of Cyprus but passed it by on our left as we continued on toward Syria. Finally we put in at Tyre, where the ship had to unload cargo.

We looked for the disciples there and stayed with them for a week. Under the Spirit's prompting, they tried to tell Paul that he should not go up to Jerusalem; but to no purpose. Then, when our time was up, we continued our journey. All of them—wives and children included—came out of the city to see us off, and we knelt down on the beach and prayed. After we had said good-bye to one another, we boarded the ship and they returned home.

Continuing our voyage from Tyre we put in at Ptolemais, where we greeted the brothers and spent the day with them. The next day we pushed on and came to Caesarea. There we entered the home of Philip the evangelist, one of the Seven, with whom we stayed. This man had four unmarried daughters gifted with prophecy. During our few days' stay, a prophet named Agabus arrived from Judea. He came up to us, and taking Paul's belt, tied his own hands and feet with it. Then he said, "Thus says the Holy Spirit: 'This is how the Jews in Jerusalem will bind the owner of this belt and hand him over to the Gentiles.' " Upon hearing this, both we ourselves and the people of Caesarea urged Paul not to proceed to Jerusalem. He answered with a question: "Why are you crying and breaking my heart in this way? For the name of the Lord Jesus I am prepared, not only for imprisonment, but for death, in Jerusalem." Since he would not be dissuaded, we said nothing further except, "The Lord's will be done."

PAUL IN ROME

Paul added one final word: "The Holy Spirit stated it well . . . 'You listen . . . yet you will never understand'"

Acts 28:16-31

This is how we finally came to Rome. Certain brothers from Rome who heard about us came out as far as the Forum of Appius and the Three Taverns to meet us. When Paul saw them, he thanked God and took fresh courage. Upon our entry into Rome Paul was allowed to take a lodging of his own, although a soldier was assigned to keep guard over him.

Three days later Paul invited the prominent men of the Jewish community to visit him. When they had gathered he said: "My brothers, I have done nothing against our people or our ancestral customs; yet in Jerusalem I was handed over to the Romans as a prisoner. The Romans tried my case and wanted to release me because they found nothing against me deserving of death. When the Jews objected, I was forced to appeal to the emperor, though I had no cause to make accusations against my own people. This is the reason, then, why I have asked to see you and speak with you. I wear these chains solely because I share the hope of Israel."

They replied: "We have had no letters from Judea about you, nor have any of the brothers arrived with a report or rumor to your discredit. For our part, we are anxious to hear you present your views. We know very well that this sect is denounced everywhere."

With that, they arranged a day with him and came to his lodgings in great numbers. From morning to evening he laid the case before them, bearing witness to the reign of God among men. He sought to convince them about Jesus by appealing to the law of Moses and the prophets. Some, indeed, were convinced by what he said; others would not believe.

Without reaching any agreement among themselves, they began to leave. Then Paul added one final word: "The Holy Spirit stated it well when he said to your fathers through the prophet Isaiah:

'Go to this people and say:
  You may listen carefully yet you will never
      understand;
    you may look intently yet you will never see.
  The heart of this people has grown sluggish.
  They have scarcely used their ears to listen;
    their eyes they have closed,
  Lest they should see with their eyes,
    hear with their ears,
    understand with their minds,
  And repent;
    and I should have to heal them.'

Now you must realize that this salvation of God has been transmitted to the Gentiles—who will heed it!"

PART IV

THE SPIRIT IN THE EPISTLES OF PAUL

1. Romans

SPIRITUAL CIRCUMCISION

. . . true circumcision is of the heart; its source is the spirit . . .

Rm 2:25-29

Circumcision, to be sure, has value if you observe the law, but if you break it you might as well be uncircumcised! Again, if an uncircumcised person keeps the precepts of the law, will he not be considered circumcised? If a man who is uncircumcised keeps the law, he will pass judgment on you who, with your written law and circumcision, break it. Appearance does not make a Jew. True circumcision is not a sign in the flesh. He is a real Jew who is one inwardly, and true circumcision is of the heart; its source is the spirit,* not the letter. Such a one receives his praise, not from men, but from God.

---

*ABS reads: . . . is the work of God's Spirit . . .

WE ARE GOD'S FRIENDS

*. . . because the love of God has been poured out
in our hearts through the Holy Spirit . . .*

Rm 5:1-11

Now that we have been justified by faith, we are at peace
with God through our Lord Jesus Christ. Through
him we have gained access by faith to the grace in
which we now stand, and we boast of our hope for the
glory of God. But not only that—we even boast of our
afflictions! We know that affliction makes for endurance,
and endurance for tested virtue, and tested virtue for
hope. And this hope will not leave us disappointed,
because the love of God has been poured out in our
hearts through the Holy Spirit who has been given to
us. At the appointed time, when we were still powerless,
Christ died for us godless men. It is rare that anyone
should lay down his life for a just man, though it is
barely possible that for a good man someone may have
the courage to die. It is precisely in this that God proves
his love for us: that while we were still sinners, Christ
died for us. Now that we have been justified by his
blood, it is all the more certain that we shall be saved by
him from God's wrath. For if, when we were God's
enemies, we were reconciled to him by the death of his
Son, it is all the more certain that we who have been
reconciled will be saved by his life. Not only that; we
go so far as to make God our boast through our Lord
Jesus Christ, through whom we have now received
reconciliation.

. . . we serve in the new life of the Spirit . . .

Rm 7:1-6

Are you not aware, my brothers (I am speaking to men who know what law is), that the law has power over a man only so long as he lives? For example, a married woman is bound to her husband by law while he lives, but if he dies she is released from the law regarding husbands. She will be called an adulteress if, while her husband is still alive, she gives herself to another. But if her husband dies she is freed from that law, and does not commit adultery by consorting with another man. In the same way, my brothers, you died to the law through the body of Christ, that you might belong to that Other who was raised from the dead, so that we might bear fruit for God. When we were in the flesh, the sinful passions roused by the law worked in our members and we bore fruit for death. Now we have been released from the law —for we have died to what bound us—and we serve in the new spirit,* not the antiquated letter.

LIFE IN THE SPIRIT

All who are led by the Spirit of God are the sons of God

Rm 8:1-17

There is no condemnation now for those who are in Christ Jesus. The law of the spirit, the spirit of life in Christ Jesus, has freed you from the law of sin and death. The law was powerless because of its weakening by the

---

*RSV reads: . . . in the new life of the Spirit . . .

flesh. Then God sent his Son in the likeness of sinful flesh as a sin offering, thereby condemning sin in the flesh, so that the just demands of the law might be fulfilled in us who live, not according to the flesh, but according to the spirit. Those who live according to the flesh are intent on the things of the flesh, those who live according to the spirit, on those of the spirit. The tendency of the flesh is toward death but that of the spirit toward life and peace. The flesh in its tendency is at enmity with God; it is not subject to God's law. Indeed, it cannot be; those who are in the flesh cannot please God. But you are not in the flesh; you are in the spirit, since the Spirit of God dwells in you. If anyone does not have the Spirit of Christ, he does not belong to Christ. If Christ is in you the body is indeed dead because of sin, while the spirit lives because of justice. If the Spirit of him who raised Jesus from the dead dwells in you, then he who raised Christ from the dead will bring your mortal bodies to life also through his Spirit dwelling in you.

We are debtors, then, my brothers—but not to the flesh, so that we should live according to the flesh. If you live according to the flesh, you will die; but if by the spirit you put to death the evil deeds of the body, you will live.

All who are led by the Spirit of God are sons of God. You did not receive a spirit of slavery leading you back into fear, but a spirit of adoption through which we cry out, "Abba!" (that is, "Father"). The Spirit himself gives witness with our spirit that we are children of God. But if we are children, we are heirs as well: heirs of God, heirs with Christ, if only we suffer with him so as to be glorified with him.

THE SPIRIT IN US

. . . the Spirit himself makes intercession for us

Rm 8:18-30

I consider the sufferings of the present to be as nothing
compared with the glory to be revealed in us. Indeed,
the whole created world eagerly awaits the revelation
of the sons of God. Creation was made subject to
futility, not of its own accord but by him who once
subjected it; yet not without hope, because the world
itself will be freed from its slavery to corruption and
share in the glorious freedom of the children of God.
Yes, we know that all creation groans and is in agony
even until now. Not only that, but we ourselves, although
we have the Spirit as first fruits, groan inwardly while
we await the redemption of our bodies. In hope we were
saved. But hope is not hope if its object is seen; how is it
possible for one to hope for what he sees? And hoping
for what we cannot see means awaiting it with patient
endurance.

   The Spirit too helps us in our weakness, for we do not
know how to pray as we ought; but the Spirit himself
makes intercession for us with groanings that cannot be
expressed in speech. He who searches hearts knows what
the Spirit means, for the Spirit intercedes for the saints
as God himself wills.

My conscience bears me witness in the Holy Spirit . . .

Rm 9:1-2

I speak the truth in Christ: I do not lie. My conscience
bears me witness in the Holy Spirit that there is great
grief and constant pain in my heart.

. . . and the joy that is given by the Holy Spirit

Rm 14:17-19

The kingdom of God is not a matter of eating or
drinking, but of justice, peace, and the joy that is given
by the Holy Spirit. Whoever serves Christ in this way
pleases God and wins the esteem of men. Let us, then,
make it our aim to work for peace and to strengthen one
another.

GOD'S FIDELITY AND MERCY

*. . . so that through the power of the Holy Spirit
you may have hope in abundance*

Rm 15:7-13

Accept one another, then, as Christ accepted you, for
the glory of God. Yes, I affirm that Christ became the
servant of the Jews because of God's faithfulness in
fulfilling the promises to the patriarchs whereas the
Gentiles glorify God because of his mercy. As Scripture
has it, "Therefore I will praise you among the Gentiles
and I will sing to your name." Again, "Rejoice, O
Gentiles, with his people." And, "Praise the Lord, all
you Gentiles and sing his glory, all you peoples." Once
more, Isaiah says, "The root of Jesse will appear, he who
will rise up to rule the Gentiles; in him the Gentiles will
find hope." So may God, the source of hope, fill you
with all joy and peace in believing so that through the
power of the Holy Spirit you may have hope in
abundance.

CONSECRATED BY THE HOLY SPIRIT

. . . with mighty signs and marvels, by the power of God's Spirit

Rm 15:14-21

I am convinced, my brothers, that you are filled with goodness, that you have complete knowledge, and that you are able to give advice to one another. Yet I have written to you rather boldly in parts of this letter by way of reminder. I take this liberty because God has given me the grace to be a minister of Christ Jesus among the Gentiles, with the priestly duty of preaching the gospel of God so that the Gentiles may be offered up as a pleasing sacrifice, consecrated by the Holy Spirit. This means I can take glory in Christ Jesus for the work I have done for God. I will not dare to speak of anything except what Christ has done through me to win the Gentiles to obedience by word and deed, with mighty signs and marvels, by the power of God's Spirit. As a result, I have completed preaching the gospel of Christ from Jerusalem all the way around to Illyria. It has been a point of honor with me never to preach in places where Christ's name was already known, for I did not want to build on a foundation laid by another but rather to fulfill the words of Scripture, "They who received no word of him will see him, and they who have never heard will understand."

*. . . for the sake of our Lord Jesus Christ
and the love of the Spirit . . .*

Rm 15:30-33

I beg you, brothers, for the sake of our Lord Jesus Christ
and the love of the Spirit, join me in the struggle by your
prayers to God on my behalf. Pray that I may be kept
safe from the unbelievers in Judea, and that the offerings
I bring to Jerusalem may be well received by the saints
there; so that, God willing, I may come to you with joy
and be refreshed in spirit by your company. May the
God of peace be with you all. Amen.

2. 1 Corinthians

THE POWER OF GOD'S SPIRIT

. . . (not) "wise" argumentation, but the convincing power of the Spirit

1 Cor 2:1-16

As for myself, brothers, when I came to you I did not come proclaiming God's testimony with any particular eloquence or "wisdom." No, I determined that while I was with you I would speak of nothing but Jesus Christ and him crucified. When I came among you it was in weakness and fear, and with much trepidation. My message and my preaching had none of the persuasive force of "wise" argumentation, but the convincing power of the Spirit. As a consequence, your faith rests not on the wisdom of men but on the power of God.

There is, to be sure, a certain wisdom which we express among the spiritually mature. It is not a wisdom of this age, however, nor of the rulers of this age, who are men headed for destruction. No, what we utter is God's wisdom: a mysterious, a hidden wisdom. God planned it before all ages for our glory. None of the rulers of this age knew the mystery; if they had known it, they would never have crucified the Lord of glory. Of this wisdom it is written:

"Eye has not seen, ear has not heard,
   nor has it so much as dawned on man
   what God has prepared for those who love him."

The Spirit scrutinizes all matters,
even the deep things of God

Yet God has revealed this wisdom to us through the
Spirit. The Spirit scrutinizes all matters, even the deep
things of God. Who, for example, knows a man's
innermost self but the man's own spirit within him?
Similarly, no one knows what lies at the depths of God
but the Spirit of God. The Spirit we have received is
not the world's spirit but God's Spirit, helping us to recognize the gifts he has given us. We speak of these, not
in words of human wisdom but in words taught by the
Spirit, thus interpreting spiritual things in spiritual terms.
The natural man does not accept what is taught by the
Spirit of God. For him, that is absurdity. He cannot
come to know such teaching because it must be appraised
in a spiritual way. The spiritual man, on the other hand,
can appraise everything, though he himself can be
appraised by no one. For, "Who has known the mind of
the Lord so as to instruct him?" But we have the mind
of Christ.

WE ARE GOD's CO-WORKERS

. . . I could not talk to you as spiritual men . . .

1 Cor 3:1-23

Brothers, the trouble was that I could not talk to you as
spiritual men* but only as men of flesh, as infants in
——————
*ABS reads: . . . as I talk to men who have the Spirit . . .

Christ. I fed you with milk, and did not give you solid food because you were not ready for it. You are not ready for it even now, being still very much in a natural condition. For as long as there are jealousy and quarrels among you, are you not of the flesh? And is not your behavior that of ordinary men? When someone says, "I belong to Paul," and someone else, "I belong to Apollos," is it not clear that you are still at the human level?

After all, who is Apollos? And who is Paul? Simply ministers through whom you became believers, each of them doing only what the Lord assigned him. I planted the seed and Apollos watered it, but God made it grow. This means that neither he who plants nor he who waters is of any special account, only God, who gives the growth. He who plants and he who waters work to the same end. Each will receive his wages in proportion to his toil. We are God's co-workers, while you are his cultivation, his building.

Are you not aware that you are the temple of God and the Spirit of God dwells in you?

Thanks to the favor God showed me I laid a foundation as a wise master-builder might do, and now someone else is building upon it. Everyone, however, must be careful how he builds. No one can lay a foundation other than the one that has been laid, namely Jesus Christ. If different ones build on this foundation with gold, silver, precious stones, wood, hay or straw, the work of each will be made clear. The Day will disclose it. That day will make its appearance with fire, and fire will test the quality of each man's work. If the building a

man has raised on this foundation still stands, he will
receive his recompense; if a man's building burns, he will
suffer loss. He himself will be saved, but only as one
fleeing through fire.

Are you not aware that you are the temple of God,
and that the Spirit of God dwells in you? If anyone
destroys God's temple, God will destroy him. For the
temple of God is holy, and you are that temple.

Let no one delude himself. If any one of you thinks
he is wise in a worldly way, he had better become a fool.
In that way he will really be wise, for the wisdom of this
world is absurdity with God. Scripture says, "He catches
the wise in their craftiness"; and again, "The Lord
knows how empty are the thoughts of the wise." Let
there be no boasting about men. All things are yours,
whether it be Paul, or Apollos, or Cephas, or the world,
or life, or death, or the present, or the future: all these
are yours, and you are Christ's, and Christ is God's.

A TEMPLE OF THE HOLY SPIRIT

*You must know that your body is a temple
of the Holy Spirit . . .*

1 Cor 6:9-20

Can you not realize that the unholy will not fall heir
to the kingdom of God? Do not deceive yourselves: no
fornicators, idolaters, or adulterers, no sodomites, thieves,
misers, or drunkards, no slanderers or robbers will inherit
God's kingdom. And such were some of you; but you
have been washed, consecrated, justified in the name of
our Lord Jesus Christ and in the Spirit of our God.

"Everything is lawful for me"—but that does not
mean that everything is good for me. "Everything is

lawful for me"—but I will not let myself be enslaved by
anything. "Food is for the stomach and the stomach for
food, and God will do away with them both in the end"—
but the body is not for immorality; it is for the Lord, and
the Lord is for the body. God, who raised up the Lord,
will raise us also by his power.

Do you not see that your bodies are members of
Christ? Would you have me take Christ's members and
make them the members of a prostitute? God forbid!
Can you not see that the man who is joined to a prostitute
becomes one body with her? Scripture says, "The two
shall become one flesh." But whoever is joined to the
Lord becomes one spirit with him. Shun lewd conduct.
Every other sin a man commits is outside his body, but
the fornicator sins against his own body. You must
know that your body is a temple of the Holy Spirit, who
is within—the Spirit you have received from God. You
are not your own. You have been purchased, and at a
price. So glorify God in your body.

WIDOWS

*I am persuaded that in this I have
the Spirit of God*

1 Cor 7:39-40

A wife is bound to her husband as long as he lives. If
her husband dies she is free to marry, but on one condition, that it be in the Lord. She will be happier, though,
in my opinion, if she stays unmarried. I am persuaded
that in this I have the Spirit of God.

GIFTS OF THE SPIRIT

There are different gifts but the same Spirit

1 Cor 12:1-11

Now, brothers, I do not want to leave you in ignorance about spiritual gifts. You know that when you were pagans you were led astray to mute idols, as impulse drove you. That is why I tell you that nobody who speaks in the Spirit of God ever says, "Cursed be Jesus." And no one can say: "Jesus is Lord," except in the Holy Spirit.

There are different gifts but the same Spirit; there are different ministries but the same Lord; there are different works but the same God who accomplishes all of them in everyone. To each person the manifestation of the Spirit is given for the common good. To one the Spirit gives wisdom in discourse, to another the power to express knowledge. Through the Spirit one receives faith; by the same Spirit another is given the gift of healing and still another miraculous powers. Prophecy is given to one; to another power to distinguish one spirit from another. One receives the gift of tongues, another that of interpreting the tongues. But it is one and the same Spirit who produces all these gifts, distributing them to each as he wills.

SET YOUR HEARTS ON THE GREATER GIFTS

All of us have been given to drink of one Spirit

1 Cor 12:12-31

The body is one and has many members, but all the members, many though they are, are one body; and so it is with Christ. It was in one Spirit that all of us, whether Jew or Greek, slave or free, were baptized into one body. All of us have been given to drink of the one Spirit. Now the body is not one member, it is many. If the foot should say, "Because I am not a hand I do not belong to the body," would it then no longer belong to the body? If the ear should say, "Because I am not an eye I do not belong to the body," would it then no longer belong to the body? If the body were all eye, what would happen to our hearing? If it were all ear, what would happen to our smelling? As it is, God has set each member of the body in the place he wanted it to be. If all the members were alike, where would the body be? There are, indeed, many different members, but one body. The eye cannot say to the hand, "I do not need you," any more than the head can say to the feet, "I do not need you." Even those members of the body which seem less important are in fact indispensable. We honor the members we consider less honorable by clothing them with greater care, thus bestowing on the less presentable a propriety which the more presentable already have. God has so constructed the body as to give greater honor to the lowly members, that there may be no dissension in the body, but that all the members may be concerned for one another. If one member suffers, all the members suffer with it; if one member is honored, all the members share its joy.

You, then, are the body of Christ. Every one of you is a member of it. Furthermore, God has set up in the church first apostles, second prophets, third teachers, then miracle workers, healers, assistants, administrators, and those who speak in tongues. Are all apostles? Are all prophets? Are all teachers? Do all work miracles or have the gift of healing? Do all speak in tongues, all have the gift of interpretation of tongues? Set your hearts on the greater gifts.

THE SURPASSING GIFT OF THE SPIRIT

. . . and the greatest of these is love

1 Cor 13:1-13

Now I will show you the way which surpasses all the others. If I speak with human tongues and angelic as well, but do not have love, I am a noisy gong, a clanging cymbal. If I have the gift of prophecy and, with full knowledge, comprehend all mysteries, if I have faith great enough to move mountains, but have not love, I am nothing. If I give everything I have to feed the poor and hand over my body to be burned, but have not love, I gain nothing.

Love is patient; love is kind. Love is not jealous, it does not put on airs, it is not snobbish. Love is never rude, it is not self-seeking, it is not prone to anger; neither does it brood over injuries. Love does not rejoice in what is wrong but rejoices with the truth. There is no limit to love's forbearance, to its trust, its hope, its power to endure.

Love never fails. Prophecies will cease, tongues will be silent, knowledge will pass away. Our knowledge is imperfect and our prophesying is imperfect. When the perfect comes, the imperfect will pass away. When I was a child I used to talk like a child, think like a child, reason like a child. When I became a man I put childish ways aside. Now we see indistinctly, as in a mirror; then we shall see face to face. My knowledge is imperfect now; then I shall know even as I am known. There are in the end three things that last: faith, hope, and love, and the greatest of these is love.

MORE ABOUT THE GIFTS OF THE SPIRIT

Set your heart on spiritual gifts. . . .

1 Cor 14:1-40

Gift of Prophecy
Seek eagerly after love. Set your hearts on spiritual
gifts—above all, the gift of prophecy. A man who speaks
in a tongue is talking not to men but to God. No one
understands him, because he utters mysteries in the Spirit.
The prophet, on the other hand, speaks to men for
their upbuilding, their encouragement, their consolation.
He who speaks in a tongue builds up himself, but he who
prophesies builds up the church. I should like it if all of
you spoke in tongues, but I much prefer that you
prophesy. The prophet is greater than one who speaks in
tongues, unless the speaker can also interpret for the
upbuilding of the church.

Interpretation of Tongues
Just suppose, brothers, that I should come to you speaking in tongues. What good will I do you if my speech
does not have some revelation, or knowledge, or
prophecy, or instruction for you? Even in the case of
lifeless things which produce a sound, such as a flute or a
harp, how will anyone know what is being played if there
is no distinction among the notes? If the bugle's sound
is uncertain, who will get ready for battle? Similarly, if
you do not utter intelligible speech because you are
speaking in a tongue, how will anyone know what you
are saying? You will be talking to the air. There are
many different languages in the world and all are marked
by sound; but if I do not know the meaning, I shall be

a foreigner to the speaker and he a foreigner to me. Since you have set your hearts on spiritual gifts, try to be rich in those that build up the church.

This means that the man who speaks in a tongue should pray for the gift of interpretation. If I pray in a tongue my spirit is at prayer but my mind contributes nothing. What is my point here? I want to pray with my spirit, and also to pray with my mind. I want to sing with my spirit and with my mind as well.

If your praise of God is solely with the spirit, how will the one who does not comprehend be able to say "Amen" to your thanksgiving? He will not know what you are saying. You will be uttering praise very well indeed, but the other man will not be helped. Thank God, I speak in tongues more than any of you, but in the church I would rather say five intelligible words to instruct others than ten thousand words in a tongue.

Function of These Gifts

Brothers, do not be childish in your outlook. Be like children as far as evil is concerned, but in mind be mature. It is written in the law, "In strange tongues and in alien speech I will speak to this people, and even so they will not heed me, says the Lord." The gift of tongues is a sign, not for those who believe but for those who do not believe, while prophecy is not for those who are without faith but for those who have faith. If the uninitiated or unbelievers should come in when the whole church is assembled and everyone is speaking in tongues, would they not say that you are out of your minds? But if an unbeliever or an uninitiate enters while all are uttering prophecy, he will be taken to task by all and called to account by all, and the secret of his heart will be laid bare. Falling prostrate, he will worship God, crying out, "God is truly among you."

174

Purpose and order

What do we propose, brothers? When you assemble, one has a psalm, another some instruction to give, still another a revelation to share; one speaks in a tongue, another interprets. All well and good, so long as everything is done with a constructive purpose. If any are going to talk in tongues let it be at most two or three, each in turn, with another to interpret what they are saying. But if there is no one to interpret, there should be silence in the assembly, each one speaking only to himself and to God. Let no more than two or three prophets speak, and let the rest judge the worth of what they say. If another, sitting by, should happen to receive a revelation, the first ones should then keep quiet.

You can all speak your prophecies, but one by one, so that all may be instructed and encouraged. The spirits of the prophets are under the prophets' control, since God is a God, not of confusion, but of peace.

If anyone thinks he is a prophet or a man of the Spirit, he should know that what I have written you is the Lord's commandment. If anyone ignores it, he in turn should be ignored. Set your hearts on prophecy, my brothers, and do not forbid those who speak in tongues, but make sure that everything is done properly and in order.

THE RESURRECTION OF THE BODY

. . . the last Adam has become a life-giving spirit

1 Cor 15:35-49

Perhaps someone will say "How are the dead to be
raised up? What kind of body will they have?" A
nonsensical question! The seed you sow does not
germinate unless it dies. When you sow, you do not sow
the full-blown plant, but a kernel of wheat or some
other grain. God gives body to it as he pleases—to each
seed its own fruition. Not all bodily nature is the same.
Men have one kind of body, animals another. Birds are
of their kind, fish are of theirs. There are heavenly bodies
and there are earthly bodies. The splendor of the
heavenly bodies is one thing, that of the earthly another.
The sun has a splendor of its own, so has the moon, and
the stars have theirs. Even among the stars, one differs
from another in brightness. So is it with the resurrection
of the dead. What is sown in the earth is subject to
decay, what rises is incorruptible. What is sown is
ignoble, what rises is glorious. Weakness is sown,
strength rises up. A natural body is put down and a
spiritual body comes up. If there is a natural body, be
sure there is also a spiritual body. Scripture has it that
Adam, the first man, became a living soul; the last
Adam has become a life-giving spirit.* Take note, the
spiritual was not first; first came the natural and after
that the spiritual. The first man was of earth, formed
from dust, the second is from heaven. Earthly men are
like the man of earth, heavenly men are like the man of
heaven. Just as we resemble the man from earth, so shall
we bear the likeness of the man from heaven.

———
*ABS reads: the last Adam is the life-giving Spirit

3. 2 Corinthians

. . . he has sealed us, thereby depositing the
first payment, the Spirit, in our hearts

2 Cor 1:18-22

As God keeps his word, I declare that my word to you
is not "yes" one minute and "no" the next. Jesus Christ,
whom Silvanus, Timothy, and I preached to you as Son
of God, was not alternately "yes" and "no"; he was
never anything but "yes." Whatever promises God has
made have been fulfilled in him; therefore it is through
him that we address our Amen to God when we worship
together. God is the one who firmly establishes us along
with you in Christ; it is he who anointed us and has
sealed us, thereby depositing the first payment, the
Spirit, in our hearts.*

---

*RSV reads: . . . he has put his seal upon us and given us his
Spirit in our hearts as a guarantee

177

A COVENANT OF THE SPIRIT

The written law kills, but the Spirit gives life

2 Cor 3:1-18

Am I beinning to speak well of myself again? Or do I
need letters of recommendation to you or from you as
others might? You are my letter, known and read by all
men, written on your hearts. Clearly you are a letter of
Christ which I have delivered, a letter written not with
ink but by the Spirit of the living God, not on tablets
of stone but on tablets of flesh in the heart.

   This great confidence in God is ours, through Christ.
It is not that we are entitled of ourselves to take credit
for anything. Our sole credit is from God, who has made
us qualified ministers of a new covenant, a covenant not
of a written law but of spirit. The written law kills, but
the Spirit gives life.

   If the ministry of death, carved in writing on stone,
was inaugurated with such glory that the Israelites could
not look on Moses' face because of the glory that shone
on it (even though it was a fading glory), how much
greater will be the glory of the ministry of the Spirit? If
the ministry of the covenant that condemned had glory,
greater by far is the glory of the ministry that justifies.
Indeed, when you compare that limited glory with this
surpassing glory, the former should be declared no glory
at all. If what was destined to pass away was given in
glory, greater by far is the glory that endures.

. . . the Lord is the Spirit . . .

Our hope being such, we speak with full confidence.
We are not like Moses, who used to hide his face with
a veil so that the Israelites could not see the final fading

of that glory. Their minds, of course, were dulled. To this very day, when the old covenant is read the veil remains unlifted; it is only in Christ that it is taken away. Even now, when Moses is read a veil covers their understanding. "But whenever he turns to the Lord, the veil will be removed." The Lord is the Spirit, and where the Spirit of the Lord is, there is freedom. All of us, gazing on the Lord's glory with unveiled faces, are being transformed from glory to glory into his very image by the Lord who is the Spirit.

LIVING BY FAITH

God . . . has given us the Spirit as a pledge of it

2 Cor 4:13-5:5

We have that spirit of faith of which the Scripture says, "Because I believed, I spoke out." We believe and so we speak, knowing that he who raised up the Lord Jesus will raise us up along with Jesus and place both us and you in his presence. Indeed, everything is ordered to your benefit, so that the grace bestowed in abundance may bring greater glory to God because they who give thanks are many.

We do not lose heart, because our inner being is renewed each day even though our body is being destroyed at the same time. The present burden of our trial is light enough, and earns for us an eternal weight of glory beyond all comparison. We do not fix our gaze on what is seen but on what is unseen. What is seen is transitory; what is unseen lasts forever.

Indeed, we know that when the earthly tent in which we dwell is destroyed we have a dwelling provided for us by God, a dwelling in the heavens, not made by hands but to last forever. We groan while we are here, even as we yearn to have our heavenly habitation envelop us. This it will, provided we are found clothed and not naked. While we live in our present tent we groan; we are weighed down because we do not wish to be stripped naked but rather to have the heavenly dwelling envelop us, so that what is mortal may be absorbed by life. God has fashioned us for this very thing and has given us the Spirit as a pledge of it.

NOW IS THE TIME

. . . conducting ourselves with innocence, knowledge, and patience, in the Holy Spirit . . .

2 Cor 6:3-10

As your fellow workers we beg you not to receive the grace of God in vain. For he says, "In an acceptable time I have heard you; on a day of salvation I have helped you." Now is the acceptable time! Now is the day of salvation! We avoid giving anyone offense, so that our ministry may not be blamed. On the contrary, in all that we do we strive to present ourselves as ministers of God, acting with patient endurance amid trials, difficulties, distresses, beatings, imprisonments, and riots; as men familiar with hard work, sleepless nights, and fastings; conducting ourselves with innocence, knowledge, and patience, in the Holy Spirit, in sincere love; as men with the message of truth and the power of God; wielding the weapons of righteousness with right hand and left, whether honored or dishonored, spoken of well or ill. We are called imposters, yet we are truthful; nobodies who in fact are well known; dead, yet here we are, alive; punished, but not put to death; sorrowful, though we are always rejoicing; poor, yet we enrich many. We seem to have nothing, yet everything is ours!

. . . you accept a spirit . . . different from the Spirit . . . you received from us!

2 Cor 11:1-4

You must endure a little of my folly. Put up with me, I beg you! I am jealous of you with the jealousy of God himself, since I have given you in marriage to one husband, presenting you as a chaste virgin to Christ. My fear is that, just as the serpent seduced Eve by his cunning, your thoughts may be corrupted and you may fall away from your sincere and complete devotion to Christ. I say this because, when someone comes preaching another Jesus than the one we preached, or when you receive a different spirit than the one you have received, or a gospel other than the gospel you accepted,* you seem to endure it quite well.

FAREWELL

. . . and the fellowship of the Holy Spirit be with you all!

2 Cor 13:10-13

I am writing in this way while away from you, so that when I am with you I may not have to exercise with severity the authority the Lord has given me—authority to build up rather than to destroy. And now, brothers, I must say good-bye. Mend your ways. Encourage one another. Live in harmony and peace, and the God of love and peace will be with you. Greet one another with a holy kiss. All the holy ones send greetings to you. The grace of the Lord Jesus Christ, and the love of God, and the fellowship of the Holy Spirit be with you all!

------
*ABS reads: . . . and you accept a spirit and a gospel completely different from the Spirit and the gospel you received from us!

4. Galatians

YOU SENSELESS GALATIANS

I want to learn only one thing from you:
How did you receive the Spirit?

Gal 3:1-14

You senseless Galatians! Who has cast a spell over you—
you before whose eyes Jesus Christ was displayed to view
upon his cross? I want to learn only one thing from
you: how did you receive the Spirit? Was it through
observance of the law or through faith in what you
heard? How could you be so stupid? After beginning
in the spirit, are you now to end in the flesh? Have you
had such remarkable experiences all to no purpose—if
indeed they were to no purpose? Is it because you
observe the law or because you have faith in what you
heard that God lavishes the Spirit on you and works
wonders in your midst? Consider the case of Abraham:
he "believed God, and it was credited to him as justice."
This means that those who believe are sons of Abraham.
Because Scripture saw in advance that God's way of
justifying the Gentiles would be through faith, it foretold
this good news to Abraham: "All nations shall be blessed
in you." Thus it is that all who believe are blessed along
with Abraham, the man of faith.

. . . thereby making it possible for us to receive
the promised Spirit through faith

All who depend on observance of the law, on the other
hand, are under a curse. It is written, "Cursed is he
who does not abide by everything written in the book
of the law and carry it out." It should be obvious that
no one is justified in God's sight by the law, for "the just
man shall live by faith." But the law does not depend
on faith. Its terms are: "Whoever does these things shall
live by them." Christ has delivered us from the power
of the law's curse by himself becoming a curse for us,
as it is written: "Accursed is anyone who is hanged on
a tree." This has happened so that through Christ Jesus
the blessing bestowed on Abraham might descend on the
Gentiles in Christ Jesus, thereby making it possible for
us to receive the promised Spirit through faith.

ABBA, FATHER

. . . God has sent forth in our hearts the
spirit of his Son . . .

Gal 4:6-7

The proof that you are sons is the fact that God has
sent forth into our hearts the spirit of his Son which
cries out "Abba!" ("Father!") You are no longer a
slave but a son! And the fact that you are a son makes
you an heir, by God's design.

*. . . the son born in nature's course persecuted
the one whose birth was in the realm of the spirit . . .*

Gal 4:28-29

You, my brothers, are children of the promise, as Isaac
was. But just as in those days the son born in nature's
course persecuted the one whose birth was in the realm
of spirit,* so do we find it now.

*It is in the spirit that we eagerly await the
justification we hope for . . .*

Gal 5:1-6

It was for liberty that Christ freed us. So stand firm,
and do not take on yourselves the yoke of slavery a
second time! Pay close attention to me, Paul, when I tell
you that if you have yourselves circumcised, Christ will
be of no use to you! I point out once more to all who
receive circumcision that they are bound to the law in
its entirety. Any of you who seek your justification in the
law have severed yourselves from Christ and fallen from
God's favor! It is in the spirit that we eagerly await the
justification we hope for, and only faith can yield it. In
Christ Jesus neither circumcision nor the lack of it counts
for anything; only faith, which expresses itself through
love.

---

*ABS reads: . . . the one who was born because of God's Spirit

THE FRUIT OF THE SPIRIT

Since we live by the spirit, let us follow
the spirit's lead

Gal 5:16-26

My point is that you should live in accord with the spirit
and you will not yield to the cravings of the flesh. The
flesh lusts against the spirit and the spirit against the
flesh; the two are directly opposed. This is why you do
not do what your will intends. If you are guided by
the spirit, you are not under the law. It is obvious what
proceeds from the flesh: lewd conduct, impurity,
licentiousness, idolatry, sorcery, hostilities, bickering,
jealousy, outbursts of rage, selfish rivalries, dissensions,
factions, envy, drunkenness, orgies, and the like. I
warn you, as I have warned you before: those who do
such things will not inherit the kingdom of God!
    In contrast, the fruit of the spirit is love, joy, peace,
patient endurance, kindness, generosity, faith, mildness,
and chastity. Against such there is no law! Those
who belong to Christ Jesus have crucified their flesh
with its passions and desires. Since we live by the spirit,
let us follow the spirit's lead. Let us never be boastful,
or challenging, or jealous toward one another.

. . . you who live by the spirit should gently set him
right . . .

Gal 6:1-5

My brothers, if someone is detected in sin, you who
live by the spirit should gently set him right, each of you
trying to avoid falling into temptation himself. Help

carry one another's burden; in that way you will fulfill the law of Christ. If anyone thinks he amounts to something, when in fact he is nothing, he is only deceiving himself. Each man should look to his conduct; if he has reason to boast of anything, it will be because the achievement is his and not another's. Everyone should bear his own responsibility.

. . . if the seed-ground is the spirit, he will reap everlasting life

Gal 6:7-10

The man instructed in the word should share all he has with his instructor. Make no mistake about it, no one makes a fool of God! A man will reap only what he sows. If he sows in the field of the flesh, he will reap a harvest of corruption; but if his seed-ground is the spirit, he will reap everlasting life. Let us not grow weary of doing good; if we do not relax our efforts, in due time we shall reap our harvest. While we have the opportunity, let us do good to all men—but especially those of the household of the faith.

5. Ephesians

THE FATHER'S PLAN OF SALVATION

. . . you were sealed with the Holy Spirit, who had been promised

Eph 1:3-14

Praised be the God and Father of our Lord Jesus Christ, who has bestowed on us in Christ every spiritual blessing in the heavens! God chose us in him before the world began, to be holy and blameless in his sight, to be full of love; he likewise predestined us through Christ Jesus to be his adopted sons—such was his will and pleasure—that all might praise the glorious favor he has bestowed on us in his beloved.

It is in Christ and through his blood that we have been redeemed and our sins forgiven, so immeasurably generous is God's favor to us. God has given us the wisdom to understand fully the mystery, the plan he was pleased to decree in Christ, to be carried out in the fullness of time: namely, to bring all things in the heavens and on earth into one under Christ's headship. In him we were chosen; for in the decree of God,

187

who administers everything according to his will and counsel, we were predestined to praise his glory by being the first to hope in Christ. In him you too were chosen; when you heard the glad tidings of salvation, the word of truth, and believed in it, you were sealed with the Holy Spirit who had been promised. He is the pledge of our inheritance, the first payment against the full redemption of a people God has made his own, to praise his glory.

May the God of our Lord Jesus Christ grant you a spirit of wisdom and of insight to know him clearly

Eph 1:15-23

For my part, from the time I first heard of your faith in the Lord Jesus and your love for all the members of the church, I have never stopped thanking God for you and recommending you in my prayers. May the God of our Lord Jesus Christ, the Father of glory, grant you a spirit of wisdom and insight to know him clearly. May he enlighten your innermost vision that you may know the great hope to which he has called you, the wealth of his glorious heritage to be distributed among the members of the church, and the immeasurable scope of his power in us who believe. It is like the strength he showed in raising Christ from the dead and seating him at his right hand in heaven, high above every principality, power, virtue, and domination, and every name that can be given in this age or in the age to come.

He has put all things under Christ's feet and has made him, thus exalted, head of the church, which is his body: the fullness of him who fills the universe in all its parts.

UNITED IN CHRIST

. . . in him you are being built into a temple, to become a dwelling place for God in the Spirit

Eph 2:17-22

You men of Gentile stock—called "uncircumcised" by those who, in virtue of a hand-executed rite on their flesh, call themselves "circumcised"—remember that, in former times, you had no part in Christ and were excluded from the community of Israel. You were strangers to the covenant and its promise; you were without hope and without God in the world. But now in Christ Jesus you who once were far off have been brought the blood of Christ. It is he who is our peace, and who made the two of us one by breaking down the barrier of hostility that kept us apart. In his own flesh he abolished the law with its commands and precepts, to create in himself one new man from us who had been two and to make peace, reconciling both of us to God in one body through his cross, which put that enmity to death. He came and "announced the good news of peace to you who were far off, and to those who were near"; through him we both have access in one Spirit to the Father.

This means that you are strangers and aliens no longer. No, you are fellow citizens of the saints and members of the household of God. You form a building which rises on the foundation of the apostles and prophets, with Christ Jesus himself as the capstone. Through him the whole structure is fitted together and takes shape as a holy temple in the Lord; in him you are being built into this temple, to become a dwelling place for God in the Spirit.

GOD'S PLAN

. . . the mystery of Christ . . . now revealed by the Spirit to the holy apostles and prophets. . . .

Eph 3:1-6

I am sure you have heard of the ministry which God in his goodness gave me in your regard. That is why to me, Paul, a prisoner for Christ Jesus on behalf of you Gentiles, God's secret plan as I have briefly described it was revealed. When you read what I have said, you will realize that I know what I am talking about in speaking of the mystery of Christ, unknown to men in former ages but now revealed by the Spirit to the holy apostles and prophets. It is no less than this: in Christ Jesus the Gentiles are now co-heirs with the Jews, members of the same body and sharers of the promise through the preaching of the gospel.

THE LOVE OF CHRIST

May the Father strengthen you inwardly through the working of his Spirit

Eph 3:14-20

That is why I kneel before the Father from whom every family in heaven and on earth takes its name; and I pray that he will bestow on you gifts in keeping with the riches of his glory. May he strengthen you inwardly through the working of his Spirit. May Christ dwell in your hearts through faith, and may charity be the root and foundation of your life. Thus you will be able to grasp fully, with all the holy ones, the breadth and length and height and depth of Christ's love, and experience this love which surpasses all knowledge so that you may attain to the fullness of God himself.

To him whose power now at work in us can do immeasurably more than we ask or imagine—to him be glory in the church and in Christ Jesus through all generations, world without end. Amen.

THE UNITY OF THE BODY OF CHRIST

There is but one body and one Spirit . . .

Eph 4:1-16

I plead with you, then, as a prisoner for the Lord, to live a life worthy of the calling you have received, with perfect humility, meekness, and patience, bearing with one another lovingly. Make every effort to preserve the unity which has the Spirit as its origin and peace as its binding force. There is but one body and one Spirit, just as there is but one hope given all of you by your call. There is one Lord, one faith, one baptism; one God and Father of all, who is over all, and works through all, and is in all.

Each of us has received God's favor in the measure in which Christ bestows it. Thus you find Scripture saying:

"When he ascended on high, he
took a host of captives
and gave gifts to men."

"He ascended"—what does this mean but that he had first descended into the lower regions of the earth? He who descended is the very one who ascended high above the heavens, that he might fill all men with his gifts.

191

It is he who gave apostles, prophets, evangelists, pastors and teachers in roles of service for the faithful to build up the body of Christ, till we become one in faith and in the knowledge of God's Son, and form that perfect man who is Christ come to full stature.

Let us, then, be children no longer, tossed here and there, carried about by every wind of doctrine that originates in human trickery and skill in proposing error. Rather, let us profess the truth in love and grow to the full maturity of Christ the head. Through him the whole body grows, and with the proper functioning of the members joined firmly together by each supporting ligament, builds itself up in love.

Do nothing to sadden the Holy Spirit with
whom you are sealed . . .

Eph 4:29-32

Never let evil talk pass your lips; say only the good things men need to hear, things that will really help them. Do nothing to sadden the Holy Spirit with whom you were sealed against the day of redemption. Get rid of all bitterness, all passion and anger, harsh words, slander, and malice of every kind. In place of these, be kind to one another, compassionate, and mutually forgiving, just as God has forgiven you in Christ.

ALWAYS GIVE THANKS

Be filled with the Spirit, addressing one another
with psalms, hymns and inspired songs

Eph 5:15-20

Keep careful watch over your conduct. Do not act
like fools, but like thoughtful men. Make the most of
the present opportunity, for these are evil days. Do
not continue in ignorance, but try to discern the will of
the Lord. Avoid getting drunk on wine; that leads to
debauchery. Be filled with the Spirit, addressing one
another in psalms and hymns and inspired songs. Sing
praise to the Lord with all your hearts. Give thanks to
God the Father always and for everything in the name
of our Lord Jesus Christ. Defer to one another out of
reverence for Christ.

CHRISTIAN WARFARE

At every opportunity pray in the Spirit . . .

Eph 6:10-18

Finally, draw your strength from the Lord and his
mighty power. Put on the armor of God so that you
may be able to stand firm against the tactics of the devil.
Our battle is not against human forces but against the
principalities and powers, the rulers of this world of
darkness, the evil spirits in regions above. You must
put on the armor of God if you are to resist on the evil
day; do all that your duty requires, and hold your
ground. Stand fast, with the truth as the belt around
your waist, justice as your breastplate, and zeal to pro-

pagate the gospel of peace as your footgear. In all circumstances hold faith up before you as your shield; it will help you extinguish the fiery darts of the evil one. Take the helmet of salvation and the sword of the spirit, the word of God.

At every opportunity pray in the Spirit, using prayers and petitions of every sort.

6. Philippians and Colossians

"LIFE" MEANS CHRIST

. . . thanks to your prayers and the support I receive from the Spirit of Jesus Christ

Phil 1:12-21

My brothers, I want you to know that my situation has worked out to the furtherance of the gospel. My imprisonment in Christ's cause has become well known throughout the praetorium here, and to others as well; most of my brothers in Christ, taking courage from my chains, have been further emboldened to speak the word of God fearlessly. It is true, some preach Christ from motives of envy and rivalry, but others do so out of good will. Some act from unaffected love, aware that my circumstances provide an opportunity to defend the gospel's cause; others promote Christ, not from pure motives but as an intrigue against me, thinking that it will make my imprisonment even harsher.

What of it? All that matters is that in any and every way, whether from specious motives or genuine ones, Christ is being proclaimed! That is what brings me joy. Indeed, I shall continue to rejoice, in the conviction that this will turn out to my salvation, thanks to your prayers and the support I receive from the Spirit of Jesus Christ. I firmly trust and anticipate that I shall never be put to shame for my hopes; I have full confidence that now as always Christ will be exalted through me, whether I live or die. For, to me, "life" means Christ; hence dying is so much gain.

JESUS CHRIST IS LORD

In the name of . . . fellowship in spirit . . .

Phil 2:1-11

In the name of the encouragement you owe me in Christ, in the name of the solace that love can give, of fellowship in spirit,* compassion, and pity, I beg you: make my joy complete by your unanimity, possessing the one love, united in spirit and ideals. Never act out of rivalry or conceit; rather, let all parties think humbly of others as superior to themselves, each of you looking to others' interests rather than to his own.

Your attitude must be that of Christ:
Though he was in the form of God,
   he did not deem equality with God
   something to be grasped at.
Rather, he emptied himself
   and took the form of a slave,
   being born in the likeness of men.

He was known to be of human estate,
   and it was thus that he humbled himself,
   obediently accepting even death,
   death on a cross!

---

*RSV reads: So if there is any encouragement in Christ, any incentive of love, any participation in the Spirit . . .

Because of this,
  God highly exalted him
  and bestowed on him the name
  above every other name,

So that at Jesus' name
  every knee must bend
  in the heavens, on the earth,
  and under the earth,
  and every tongue proclaim
  to the glory of God the Father:
  JESUS CHRIST IS LORD!

It is we . . . who worship in the spirit of God . . .

Phil 3:1-3

For the rest, my brothers, rejoice in the Lord. I find
writing you these things no burden, and for you it is a
safeguard.

Beware of unbelieving dogs. Watch out for workers
of evil. Be on guard against those who mutilate. It is
we who are the circumcision, who worship in the spirit
of God and glory in Christ Jesus rather than putting
our trust in the flesh.

PRAYER OF THANKSGIVING

He it was who told us of your love in the Spirit

Col 1:6-12

We always give thanks to God, the Father of our Lord
Jesus Christ, in our prayers for you because we have
heard of your faith in Christ Jesus and the love you
bear toward all the saints—moved as you are by the

hope held in store for you in heaven. You heard of this hope through the message of truth, the gospel, which has come to you, has borne fruit, and has continued to grow in your midst, as it has everywhere in the world. This has been the case from the day you first heard it and comprehended God's gracious intention through the instructions of Epaphras, our dear fellow slave, who represents us as a faithful minister of Christ. He it was who told us of your love in the Spirit.

Ever since we heard this we have been praying for you unceasingly and asking that you may attain full knowledge of his will through perfect wisdom and spiritual insight.*

Then you will lead a life worthy of the Lord and pleasing to him in every way. You will multiply good works of every sort and grow in the knowledge of God. By the might of his glory you will be endowed with the strength needed to stand fast, even to endure joyfully whatever may come, giving thanks to the Father for having made you worthy to share the lot of the saints in light.

---

*ABS reads: We ask God to fill you with the knowledge of his will, with all the wisdom and understanding that his Spirit gives.

7. Thessalonians

. . . with the joy that comes from the Holy Spirit

1 Thes 1:5-6

Our preaching of the gospel provided not a mere matter
of words for you but one of power; it was carried on
in the Holy Spirit and out of complete conviction. You
know as well as we do what we proved to be like when,
while still among you, we acted on your behalf. You,
in turn, became imitators of us and of the Lord,
receiving the word despite great trials, with the joy
that comes from the Holy Spirit.

CHASTITY AND CHARITY

. . . whoever rejects these instructions rejects not man,
but God who sends his Holy Spirit upon you

1 Thes 4:1-8

Now, my brothers, we beg and exhort you in the Lord
Jesus that even as you learned from us how to conduct
yourselves in a way pleasing to God—which you are
indeed doing—so you must learn to make still greater
progress. You know the instructions we gave you in

the Lord Jesus. It is God's will that you grow in holiness: that you abstain from immorality, each of you guarding his member in sanctity and honor, not in passionate desire as do the Gentiles who know not God; and that each refrain from overreaching or cheating his brother in the matter at hand; for the Lord is an avenger of all such things, as we once indicated to you by our testimony. God has not called us to immorality but to holiness, hence, whoever rejects these instructions rejects, not man, but God who sends his Holy Spirit upon you.

REJOICE ALWAYS

Do not stifle the Spirit. Do not despise prophecies

1 Thes 5:12-24

We beg you, brothers, respect those among you whose task it is to exercise authority in the Lord and admonish you; esteem them with the greatest love because of their work. Remain at peace with one another. We exhort you to admonish the unruly; cheer the fainthearted; support the weak; be patient toward all. See that no one returns evil to any other; always seek one another's good and, for that matter, the good of all.

Rejoice always, never cease praying, render constant thanks; such is God's will for you in Christ Jesus.

Do not stifle the Spirit. Do not despise prophecies. Test everything; retain what is good. Avoid any semblance of evil.

May the God of peace make you perfect in holiness. May he preserve you whole and entire, spirit, soul, and body, irreproachable at the coming of our Lord Jesus Christ. He who calls us is trustworthy, therefore he will do it.

STAND FIRM

. . . because God chose you from the beginning
to be saved through sanctification of the Spirit . . .

2 Thes 2:13-17

We are bound to thank God for you always, beloved
brothers in the Lord, because you are the first fruits
of those whom God has chosen for salvation, in holiness
of spirit* and fidelity to truth. He called you through
our preaching of the good news so that you might
achieve the glory of our Lord Jesus Christ.

    Therefore, brothers, stand firm. Hold fast to the
traditions you received from us, either by our word or
by letter. May our Lord Jesus Christ himself, may God
our Father who loved us and in his mercy gave us
eternal consolation and hope, console your hearts and
strengthen them for every good work and word.

---

*RSV reads: . . . because God chose you from the beginning to be
saved through the sanctification of the Spirit . . .

8. Timothy and Titus

THE MYSTERY OF OUR FAITH

He was manifested in the flesh, vindicated in the Spirit

1 Tm 3:14-16

Although I hope to visit you soon, I am writing you about these matters so that if I should be delayed you will know what kind of conduct befits a member of God's household, the church of the living God, the pillar and bulwark of truth. Wonderful, indeed, is the mystery of our faith, as we say in professing it:

> "He was manifested in the flesh,
>   vindicated in the Spirit;
> Seen by the angels;
>   preached among the Gentiles,
> Believed in throughout the world,
>   taken up into glory."

FALSE TEACHERS

The Spirit distinctly says that in later times
some will turn away from the faith . . .

1 Tm 4:1-5

The Spirit distinctly says that in later times some will turn away from the faith and will heed deceitful spirits and things taught by demons through plausible liars—

men with seared consciences who forbid marriage and require abstinence from foods which God created to be received with thanksgiving by believers who know the truth. Everything God created is good; nothing is to be rejected when it is received with thanksgiving, for it is made holy by God's word and by prayer.

GOOD SERVANT OF CHRIST

Do not neglect the gift you received when,
as a result of prophecy, the presbyters laid their hands
on you

1 Tm 4:6-16

If you put these instructions before the brotherhood you will be a good servant of Christ Jesus, reared in the words of faith and the sound doctrine you have faithfully followed. Have nothing to do with profane myths or old wives' tales. Train yourself for the life of piety, for while physical training is to some extent valuable, the discipline of religion is incalculably more so, with its promise of life here and hereafter. You can depend on this as worthy of complete acceptance.

This explains why we work and struggle as we do; our hopes are fixed on the living God who is the savior of all men, but especially of those who believe.

Such are the things you must urge and teach. Let no one look down on you because of your youth, but be a continuing example of love, faith, and purity to believers. Until I arrive, devote yourself to the reading of Scripture, to preaching and teaching. Do not neglect the gift you received when, as a result of prophecy, the presbyters laid their hands on you. Attend to your duties; let them absorb you, so that everyone may see your progress. Watch yourself and watch your teaching. Persevere at both tasks. By doing so you will bring to salvation yourself and all who hear you.

THE GIFT OF GOD

The Spirit God has given us is no cowardly spirit, but rather one that makes us strong . . .

2 Tm 1:3-14

I thank God, the God of my forefathers whom I worship with a clear conscience, whenever I remember you in my prayers—as indeed I do constantly, night and day. Recalling your tears when we parted, I yearn to see you again. That would make my happiness complete. I find myself thinking of your sincere faith—faith which first belonged to your grandmother Lois and to your mother Eunice, and which (I am confident) you also have.

For this reason, I remind you to stir into flame the gift of God bestowed when my hands were laid on you. The Spirit God has given us is no cowardly spirit, but rather one that makes us strong, loving, and wise. Therefore, never be ashamed of your testimony to our Lord, nor of me, a prisoner for his sake; but with the strength which comes from God bear your share of the hardship which the gospel entails.

God has saved us and has called us to a holy life, not because of any merit of ours but according to his own design—the grace held out to us in Christ Jesus before the world began but now made manifest through the appearance of our Savior. He has robbed death of its power and has brought life and immortality into clear light through the gospel. In the service of this gospel I have been appointed preacher and apostle and teacher, and for its sake I undergo present hardships. But I am not ashamed, for I know him in whom I have believed, and I am confident that he is able to guard what has been entrusted to me until that Day. Take as a model of sound teaching what you have heard me say, in faith and love in Christ Jesus. Guard the rich deposit of faith with the help of the Holy Spirit who dwells within us.

HE LAVISHED THE SPIRIT ON US

He saved us through the baptism of new birth
and renewal by the Holy Spirit

Ti 3:1-8

Remind people to be loyally subject to the government and its officials, to obey the laws, to be ready to take on any honest employment. Tell them not to speak evil of anyone or be quarrelsome. They must be forbearing and display a perfect courtesy toward all men. We ourselves were once foolish, disobedient, and far from true faith; we were the slaves of our passions and of pleasures of various kinds. We went our way in malice and envy, hateful ourselves and hating one another. But when the kindness and love of God our Savior appeared, he saved us; not because of any righteous deeds we had done, but because of his mercy. He saved us through the baptism of new birth and renewal by the Holy Spirit. This Spirit he lavished on us through Jesus Christ our Savior, that we might be justified by his grace and become heirs, in hope, of eternal life. You can depend on this to be true.

PART V

IN THE OTHER EPISTLES AND REVELATION

1. Hebrews

GOD HAS SPOKEN

. . . by signs, miracles, varied acts of power, and distribution of the gifts of the Holy Spirit . . .

Heb 1:3-4, 2:1-4

In times past, God spoke in fragmentary and varied ways to our fathers through the prophets; in this, the final age, he has spoken to us through his Son, whom he has made heir of all things and through whom he first created the universe. This Son is the reflection of the Father's glory, the exact representation of the Father's being, and he sustains all things by his powerful word. When he had cleansed us from our sins, he took his seat at the right hand of the Majesty in heaven, as far superior to the angels as the name he has inherited is superior to theirs.

In view of this, we must attend all the more to what we have heard, lest we drift away. For if the word spoken through angels stood unchanged, and all transgression and disobedience received its due punishment, how shall we escape if we ignore a salvation as great as ours? Announced first by the Lord, it was confirmed to us by those who had heard him. God then gave witness to it by signs, miracles, varied acts of power, and distribution of the gifts of the Holy Spirit as he willed.

*. . . as the Holy Spirit says: "Today, if you should
hear his voice, harden not your hearts . . . "*

Heb 3:7-8

Wherefore, as the Holy Spirit says:

> "Today, if you should hear his voice,
> harden not your hearts as at the revolt
> in the day of testing in the desert,
> when your fathers tested and tried me,
> and saw my works for forty years.

> "Because of this I was angered with that genera-
> tion
> and I said, 'They have always been of erring
> heart,
> and have never known my ways.'

> "Thus I swore in my anger,
> 'They shall never enter into my rest.' "

*For when men have once . . . become sharers in the
Holy Spirit . . and then fallen away . . .*

Heb 6:1-6

Let us, then, go beyond the initial teaching about Christ
and advance to maturity, not laying the foundation
all over again: repentance from dead works, faith in
God, instruction about baptisms and laying-on of hands,
resurrection of the dead, and eternal judgment. And,
God permitting, we shall advance!

For when men have once been enlightened and
have tasted the heavenly gift and become sharers in the
Holy Spirit, when they have tasted the good word of
God and the powers of the age to come, and then have

fallen away, it is impossible to make them repent again, since they are crucifying the Son of God for themselves and holding him up to contempt.

THE PERFECT SACRIFICE

. . . how much more will the blood of Christ, who through the eternal spirit offered himself up unblemished to God . . .

Heb 9:6-14

These were the arrangements for worship. In performing their service the priests used to go into the outer tabernacle constantly, but only the high priest went into the inner one, and that but once a year, with the blood which he offered for himself and for the sins of the people. The Holy Spirit was showing thereby that while the first tabernacle was still standing, the way into the sanctuary had not yet been revealed. This is a symbol of the present time, in which gifts and sacrifices are offered that can never make perfect the conscience of the worshiper, but can only cleanse in matters of food and drink and various ritual washings: regulations concerning the flesh, imposed until the time of the new order.

But when Christ came as high priest of the good things which have come to be, he entered once for all into the sanctuary, passing through the greater and more perfect tabernacle not made by hands, that is, not belonging to this creation. He entered, not with the blood of goats and calves, but with his own blood, and achieved eternal redemption. For if the blood of goats and bulls and the sprinkling of a heifer's ashes can sanctify those who are defiled so that their flesh is cleansed, how much more will the blood of Christ, who through the eternal spirit offered himself up unblemished to God, cleanse our consciences from dead works to worship the living God!

The Holy Spirit attests this to us. . . .

Heb 10:11-18

By this "will," we have been sanctified through the offering of the body of Jesus Christ once for all. Every other priest stands ministering day by day, and offering again and again those same sacrifices which can never take away sins. But Jesus offered one sacrifice for sins and took his seat forever at the right hand of God; now he waits until his enemies are placed beneath his feet. By one offering he has forever perfected those who are being sanctified. The Holy Spirit attests this to us, for after saying,

> "This is the covenant I will make with them
>   after those days, says the Lord:
> I will put my laws in their hearts
>   and I will write them on their minds,"

he also says,

> "Their sins and their transgressions
>   I will remember no more."

Once these have been forgiven, there is no further offering for sin.

LET US DRAW NEAR

Do you not suppose that a much worse punishment
is due the man who . . . insults the Spirit of grace?

Heb 10:19-31

Brothers, since the blood of Jesus assures our entrance
into the sanctuary by the new and living path he has
opened up for us through the veil (the "veil" meaning
his flesh), and since we have a great priest who is over
the house of God, let us draw near in utter sincerity
and absolute confidence, our hearts sprinkled clean from
the evil which lay on our conscience and our bodies
washed in pure water. Let us hold unswervingly to our
profession which gives us hope, for he who made the
promise deserves our trust. We must consider how to
rouse each other to love and good deeds. We should
not absent ourselves from the assembly, as some do,
but encourage one another; and this all the more because
you see that the Day draws near.

If we sin willfully after receiving the truth, there
remains for us no further sacrifice for sin—only a
fearful expectation of judgment and a flaming fire to
consume the adversaries of God. Anyone who rejects
the law of Moses is put to death without mercy on the
testimony of two or three witnesses. Do you not suppose
that a much worse punishment is due the man who
disdains the Son of God, thinks the covenant-blood by
which he was sanctified to be ordinary, and insults the
Spirit of grace? We know who said,

"Vengeance is mine; I will repay,"
and
"The Lord will judge his people."

It is a fearful thing to fall into the hands of the
living God.

212

2. James and Peter

DRAW CLOSE TO GOD

*. . . the scripture says, "He yearns jealously over
the spirit which he has made to dwell in us"*

Jas 4:1-10

Where do the conflicts and disputes among you
originate? Is it not your inner cravings that make war
within your members? What you desire you do not
obtain, and so you resort to murder. You envy and
you cannot acquire, so you quarrel and fight. You do not
obtain because you do not ask. You ask and you do not
receive because you ask wrongly, with a view to
squandering what you receive on your pleasures. O you
unfaithful ones, are you not aware that love of the world
is enmity to God? A man is marked out as God's enemy
if he chooses to be the world's friend. Do you suppose
it is to no purpose that Scripture says, "The spirit he
has implanted in us tends toward jealousy"?* Yet he
bestows a greater gift, for the sake of which it is written,

"God resists the proud
but bestows his favor on the lowly."

---

*RSV reads: "He yearns jealously over the Spirit which he has
made to dwell in us"

Therefore submit to God; resist the devil and he will take flight. Draw close to God, and he will draw close to you. Cleanse your hands, you sinners; purify your hearts, you backsliders. Begin to lament, to mourn, and to weep; let your laughter be turned into mourning and your joy into sorrow. Be humbled in the sight of the Lord and he will raise you on high.

CAUSE FOR REJOICING

. . . consecrated by the Spirit to a life of obedience . . .

1 Pt 1:1-12

Peter, an apostle of Jesus Christ, to those who live as strangers scattered throughout Pontus, Galatia, Cappadocia, Asia, and Bithynia; to men chosen according to the foreknowledge of God the Father, consecrated by the Spirit to a life of obedience to Jesus Christ and purification with his blood. Favor and peace be yours in abundance.

Praised be the God and Father
of our Lord Jesus Christ,
he who in his great mercy
gave us new birth;
a birth unto hope which draws its life
from the resurrection of Jesus Christ from the dead;
a birth to an imperishable inheritance,
incapable of fading or defilement,
which is kept in heaven for you
who are guarded with God's power through faith;
a birth to a salvation which stands ready
to be revealed in the last days.

. . . what now has been proclaimed to you . . . in the
power of the Spirit sent from heaven . . .

There is cause for rejoicing here. You may for a
time have to suffer the distress of many trials; but this
is so that your faith, which is more precious than the
passing splendor of fire-tried gold, may by its genuineness
lead to praise, glory, and honor when Jesus Christ
appears. Although you have never seen him, you love
him, and without seeing you now believe in him, and
rejoice with inexpressible joy touched with glory because
you are achieving faith's goal, your salvation.
This is the salvation which the prophets carefully
searched out and examined. They prophesied the divine
favor that was destined to be yours. They investigated
the times and the circumstances which the Spirit of
Christ within them was pointing to, for he predicted the
sufferings destined for Christ and the glories that would
follow. They knew by revelation that they were
providing, not for themselves but for you, what has now
been proclaimed to you by those who preach the gospel
to you, in the power of the Holy Spirit sent from heaven.
Into these matters angels long to search.

He was put to death . . . but given life in the
realm of the spirit . . .

1 Pt 3:18-19

The reason why Christ died for sins once for all, the
just man for the sake of the unjust, was that he might
lead you to God. He was put to death insofar as
fleshly existence goes, but was given life in the realm
of the spirit. It was in the spirit also that he went to
preach to the spirits in prison.

215

. . . that . . . they might live in the spirit in the eyes
of God

1 Pt 4:6

The reason the gospel was preached even to the dead
was that, although condemned in the flesh in the eyes of
men, they might live in the spirit in the eyes of God.

BLESSINGS OF PERSECUTION

. . . for then God's spirit in its glory
has come to rest on you

1 Pt 4:12-16

Do not be surprised, beloved, that a trial by fire is oc-
curring in your midst. It is a test for you, but it should
not catch you off guard. Rejoice instead, in the measure
that you share Christ's sufferings. When his glory is
revealed, you will rejoice exultantly. Happy are you
when you are insulted for the sake of Christ, for then
God's Spirit in its glory has come to rest on you. See
to it that none of you suffers for being a murderer, a
thief, a malefactor, or a destroyer of another's rights.
If anyone suffers for being a Christian, however, he
ought not to be ashamed. He should rather glorify God
in virtue of that name.

THE NATURE OF PROPHECY

. . . men impelled by the Holy Spirit have spoken under God's influence

2 Pt 1:16-21

It was not by way of cleverly concocted myths that we taught you about the coming in power of our Lord Jesus Christ, for we were eyewitnesses of his sovereign majesty. He received glory and praise from God the Father when that unique declaration came to him out of the majestic splendor: "This is my beloved Son, on whom my favor rests." We ourselves heard this said from heaven while we were in his company on the holy mountain. Besides, we possess the prophetic message as something altogether reliable. Keep your attention closely fixed on it, as you would on a lamp shining in a dark place until the first streaks of dawn appear and the morning star rises in your hearts.

First you must understand this: there is no prophecy contained in Scripture which is a personal interpretation. Prophecy has never been put forward by man's willing it. It is rather that men impelled by the Holy Spirit have spoken under God's influence.

3. John and Jude

THE ANOINTING FROM THE HOLY ONE

. . . the anointing which you received from him remains in your hearts. This means you have no need for anyone to teach you

1 Jn 2:20-27

But you have the anointing that comes from the
    Holy One,
so that all knowledge is yours.
My reason for having written you
is not that you do not know the truth
but that you do,
and that no lie has anything in common with the truth.
Who is the liar?
He who denies that Jesus is the Christ.
He is the antichrist,
denying the Father and the Son.
Anyone who denies the Son
has no claim on the Father,
but he who acknowledges the Son
can claim the Father as well.

As for you,
let what you heard from the beginning
remain in your hearts.
If what you heard from the beginning
does remain in your hearts,
then you in turn will remain in the Son and in the Father.
He himself made us a promise
and the promise is no less than this:
eternal life.
I have written you these things
about those who try to deceive you.
As for you,
the anointing you received from him
remains in your hearts.
This means you have no need
for anyone to teach you.
Rather, as his anointing teaches you about all things
and is true—free from any lie—
remain in him
as that anointing taught you.

. . . this is how we know he remains in us:
from the Spirit that he gave us

1 Jn 3:22-24

Beloved,
if our consciences have nothing to charge us with,
we can be sure that God is with us
and that we will receive at his hands
whatever we ask.
Why? Because we are keeping his commandments
and doing what is pleasing in his sight.
His commandment is this:

we are to believe in the name of his Son, Jesus Christ,
and are to love one another as he commanded us.
Those who keep his commandments remain in him
and he in them.
And this is how we know that he remains in us:
from the Spirit that he gave us.

TESTING THE SPIRITS

This is how you can recognize God's Spirit . . .

1 Jn 4:1-6

Beloved,
do not trust every spirit,
but put the spirits to a test
to see if they belong to God,
because many false prophets have appeared in the world.
This is how you can recognize God's Spirit:
every spirit that acknowledges Jesus Christ come in the
    flesh
belongs to God,
while every spirit that fails to acknowledge him
does not belong to God.
Such is the spirit of the antichrist
which, as you have heard, is to come;
in fact, it is in the world already.
You are of God, you little ones,
and thus you have conquered the false prophets.
For there is One greater in you
than there is in the world.
Those others belong to the world;
that is why theirs is the language of the world
and why the world listens to them.
We belong to God

and anyone who has knowledge of God gives us a
    hearing,
while anyone who is not of God refuses to hear us.
Thus do we distinguish the spirit of truth
from the spirit of deception.

GOD IS LOVE

The way we know that we remain in him . . .
is that he has given us his Spirit

1 Jn 4:7-16

Beloved,
let us love one another
because love is of God;
everyone who loves is begotten of God
and has knowledge of God.
The man without love has known nothing of God,
for God is love.
God's love was revealed in our midst in this way:
he sent his only Son to the world
that we might have life through him.
Love, then, consists in this:
not that we have loved God,
but that he has loved us
and has sent his Son as an offering for our sins.
Beloved,
if God has loved us so,
we must have the same love for one another.
No one has ever seen God.
Yet if we love one another
God dwells in us,
and his love is brought to perfection in us.
The way we know we remain in him

and he in us
is that he has given us of his Spirit.
We have seen for ourselves, and can testify,
that the Father has sent the Son as savior of the world.
When anyone acknowledges that Jesus is the Son of God,
God dwells in him
and he in God.
We have come to know and to believe
    in the love God has for us.
God is love,
and he who abides in love
abides in God,
and God in him.

THE SPIRIT, THE WATER, AND THE BLOOD

It is the Spirit who testifies to this,
and the Spirit is truth

1 Jn 5:6-12

Jesus Christ it is who came
    through water and blood—
not in water only,
but in water and in blood.
It is the Spirit who testifies to this,
and the Spirit is truth.
Thus there are three that testify,
the Spirit and the water and the blood—
and these three are of one accord.
Do we not accept human testimony?
The testimony of God is much greater:
it is the testimony God has given
on his own Son's behalf.
Whoever believes in the Son of God

possesses that testimony within his heart.
Whoever does not believe God
has made God a liar
by refusing to believe in the testimony
he has given on his own Son's behalf.
The testimony is this:
God gave us eternal life,
and this life is in his Son.
Whoever possesses the Son
possesses life;
Whoever does not possess the Son of God
does not possess life.

*. . . grow strong in your holy faith through
prayer in the Holy Spirit*

Jude 17-21

Remember, beloved, all of you, the prophetic words of
the apostles of our Lord Jesus Christ; how they kept
telling you, "In the last days there will be impostors
living by their godless passions." These sensualists,
devoid of the Spirit, are causing divisions among you.
But you, beloved, grow strong in your holy faith through
prayer in the Holy Spirit. Persevere in God's love, and
welcome the mercy of our Lord Jesus Christ which
leads to life eternal.

4. The Revelation to John

GREETINGS TO THE SEVEN CHURCHES

. . . and from the seven spirits before his throne . . .

Rv 1:4-8

To the seven churches in the province of Asia: John
wishes you grace and peace—from him who is and who
was and who is to come, and from the seven spirits
before his throne, and from Jesus Christ the faithful
witness, the first-born from the dead and ruler of the
kings of earth. To him who loves us and freed us from
our sins by his own blood, who has made us a royal
nation of priests in the service of his God and Father—to
him be glory and power forever and ever! Amen.

See, he comes amid the clouds!
    Every eye shall see him,
    even of those who pierced him.
All the peoples of the earth
    shall lament him bitterly.
    So it is to be! Amen!

The Lord God says, "I am the Alpha and the Omega,
the One who is and who was and who is to come, the
Almighty!"

I was in the Spirit on the Lord's day, and I heard
behind me a loud voice like a trumpet saying, "Write
what you see . . . and send it to the seven churches"

Rv 1:9-11

First Vision
I, John, your brother, who share with you the distress
and the kingly reign and the endurance we have in
Jesus, found myself on the island called Patmos because
I proclaimed God's word and bore witness to Jesus.
On the Lord's Day I was caught up in ecstasy,* and I
heard behind me a piercing voice like the sound of a
trumpet, which said, "Write on a scroll what you now see
and send it to the seven churches: to Ephesus, Smyrna,
Pergamum, Thyatira, Sardis, Philadelphia, and Laodicea."

MESSAGE TO THE CHURCHES

"Let him who has ears heed the Spirit's word
to the churches!"

Rv 2:1, 7

To Ephesus
"To the presiding spirit of the church in Ephesus, write
this:
" 'Let him who has ears heed the Spirit's word to the
churches! I will see to it that the victor eats from the
tree of life which grows in the garden of God.'

---

*RSV reads: "I was in the Spirit on the Lord's day . . ."

225

Rv 2:8, 11

To Smyrna
"To the presiding spirit of the church in Smyrna, write this:

" 'Let him who has ears heed the Spirit's word to the churches! The victor shall never be harmed by the second death.'

Rv 2:12, 17

To Pergamum
"To the presiding spirit of the church in Pergamum, write this:

" 'Let him who has ears heed the Spirit's word to the churches! To the victor I will give the hidden manna; I will also give him a white stone upon which is inscribed a new name, to be known only by him who receives it.'

Rv 2:18, 26-29

To Thyatira
"To the presiding spirit of the church in Thyatira, write this:

" 'To the one who wins the victory, who keeps to my ways till the end, I will give authority over the nations—the same authority I received from my Father. He shall rule them with a rod of iron and shatter them like crockery; and I will give him the morning star.

" 'Let him who has ears heed the Spirit's word to the churches!'

Rv 3:1, 5-6

To Sardis
"To the presiding spirit of the church in Sardis, write this:

" 'The One who holds the seven spirits of God, the seven stars, has this to say:

" 'The victor shall go clothed in white. I will never erase his name from the book of the living, but will acknowledge him in the presence of my Father and his angels.

" 'Let him who has ears heed the Spirit's word to the churches!'

Rv 3:7, 12-13

To Philadelphia
"To the presiding spirit of the church in Philadelphia, write this:

" 'I will make the victor a pillar in the temple of my God and he shall never leave it. I will inscribe on him the name of my God and the name of the city of my God, the new Jerusalem which he will send down from heaven, and my own name which is new.

" 'Let him who has ears heed the Spirit's word to the churches!'

Rv 3:14, 20-22

To Laodicea
"To the presiding spirit of the church in Loadicea, write this:

" 'Here I stand, knocking at the door. If anyone hears me calling and opens the door, I will enter his house and have supper with him, and he with me. I will give the victor the right to sit with me on my throne, as I myself won the victory and took my seat beside my Father on his throne.

" 'Let him who has ears heed the Spirit's word to the churches.' "

VISION OF HEAVENLY WORSHIP

At once I was in the Spirit, and lo, a throne
stood in the heaven . . .

Rv 4:1-11

After this I had another vision: above me there was an open door to heaven, and I heard the trumpet-like voice which had spoken to me before. It said, "Come up here and I will show you what must take place in time to come." At once I was caught up in ecstasy.* A throne was standing there in heaven, and on the throne was seated One whose appearance had a gemlike sparkle as of jasper and carnelian. Around the throne was a rainbow as brilliant as emerald. Surrounding this throne were twenty-four other thrones upon which were seated twenty-four elders; they were clothed in white garments and had crowns of gold on their heads. From the throne came flashes of lightning and peals of thunder; before it burned seven flaming torches, the seven spirits of God. The floor around the throne was like a sea of glass that was crystal-clear.

At the very center, around the throne itself, stood four living creatures covered with eyes front and back.

---

*RSV reads: At once I was in the Spirit . . .

The first creature resembled a lion, the second an ox; the third had the face of a man, while the fourth looked like an eagle in flight. Each of the four living creatures had six wings and eyes all over, inside and out.

Day and night, without pause, they sing:

"Holy, holy, holy, is the Lord God Almighty,
He who was, and who is, and who is to come!"

Whenever these creatures give glory and honor and praise to the One seated on the throne, who lives forever and ever, the twenty-four elders fall down before the One seated on the throne, and worship him who lives forever and ever. They throw down their crowns before the throne and sing:

"O Lord our God, you are worthy
    to receive glory and honor and power!
For you have created all things;
    by your will they came to be and were made!"

The Spirit added, "Yes, they shall find rest from their labors . . ."

Rv 14:13

I heard a voice from heaven say to me: "Write this down: Happy now are the dead who die in the Lord!" The Spirit added, "Yes, they shall find rest from their labors, for their good works accompany them."

The angel then carried me away in spirit
to a desolate place . . .

Rv 17:1-6

Then one of the seven angels who were holding the seven bowls came to me and said: "Come, I will show you the judgment in store for the great harlot who sits by the waters of the deep. The kings of the earth have committed fornication with her, and the earth's inhabitants have grown drunk on the wine of her lewdness." The angel then carried me away in spirit to a desolate place where I saw a woman seated on a scarlet beast which was covered with blasphemous names. This beast had seven heads and ten horns. The woman was dressed in purple and scarlet and adorned with gold and pearls and other jewels. In her hand she held a gold cup that was filled with the abominable and sordid deeds of her lewdness. On her forehead was written a symbolic name, "Babylon the great, mother of harlots and all the world's abominations." I saw that the woman was drunk with the blood of God's holy ones and the blood of those martyred for their faith in Jesus.

WEDDING FEAST OF THE LAMB

The prophetic spirit proves itself by witnessing to Jesus

Rv 19:5-10

A voice coming from the throne cried out:
"Praise our God, all you servants, the small and the great, who revere him!"

Then I heard what sounded like the shouts of a great crowd, or the roaring of the deep, or mighty peals of thunder, as they cried:

"Alleluia!
The Lord is king,
    our God, the Almighty!
Let us rejoice and be glad,
    and give him glory!
For this is the wedding day of the Lamb;
    his bride has prepared herself for the wedding.
She has been given a dress to wear
    made of finest linen, brilliant white."

(The linen dress is the virtuous deeds of God's saints.)
The angel then said to me: "Write this down: Happy are they who have been invited to the wedding feast of the Lamb." The angel continued, "These words are true; they come from God." I fell at his feet to worship him, but he said to me, "No, get up! I am merely a fellow servant with you and your brothers who give witness to Jesus. Worship God alone. The prophetic spirit proves itself by witnessing to Jesus."

THE NEW HEAVEN AND THE NEW EARTH

He carried me away in spirit to the top of a very high mountain and showed me the holy city of Jerusalem coming down out of heaven from God

Rv 21:1-11, 22-27; 22:1-5

Then I saw new heavens and a new earth. The former heavens and the former earth had passed away, and the sea was no longer. I also saw a new Jerusalem, the holy city, coming down out of heaven from God, beautiful as a bride prepared to meet her husband. I heard a loud voice from the throne cry out: "This is God's dwelling among men. He shall dwell with them and they shall be his people and he shall be their God who is always with them. He shall wipe every tear from their eyes, and there shall be no more death or mourning, crying out or pain, for the former world has passed away."

The One who sat on the throne said to me, "See, I make all things new!" Then he said, "Write these matters down, for the words are trustworthy and true!" He went on to say: "These words are already fulfilled! I am the Alpha and the Omega, the Beginning and the End. To anyone who thirsts I will give to drink without cost from the spring of lifegiving water.* He who wins the victory shall inherit these gifts; I will be his God and he shall be my son. As for the cowards and traitors to the faith, the depraved and murderers, the fornicators and sorcerers, the idol-worshipers and deceivers of every sort—their lot is the fiery pool of burning sulphur, the second death!"

---

*This "lifegiving water" is identified as "the Spirit" in Jn 7:37-39, p. 102

The New Jerusalem

One of the seven angels who held the seven bowls filled with the seven last plagues came and said to me, "Come, I will show you the woman who is the bride of the Lamb." He carried me away in spirit to the top of a very high mountain and showed me the holy city Jerusalem coming down out of heaven from God. It gleamed with the splendor of God. . . .

I saw no temple in the city. The Lord, God the Almighty, is its temple—he and the Lamb. The city had no need of sun or moon, for the glory of God gave it light, and its lamp was the Lamb. The nations shall walk by its light; to it the kings of the earth shall bring their treasures. During the day its gates shall never be shut, and there shall be no night. The treasures and wealth of the nations shall be brought there but nothing profane shall enter it, nor anyone who is a liar or has done a detestable act. Only those shall enter whose names are inscribed in the book of the living kept by the Lamb.

the river of lifegiving water . . .

The angel then showed me the river of lifegiving water,* clear as crystal, which issued from the throne of God and of the Lamb and flowed down the middle of the streets. On either side of the river grew the trees of life which produce fruit twelve times a year, once each month; their leaves serve as medicine for the nations. Nothing deserving a curse shall be found there. The throne of God and of the Lamb shall be there, and his servants shall serve him faithfully. They shall see him face to face and bear his name on their foreheads. The night shall be no more. They will need no light from lamps or the

---

*See note on p. 232

sun, for the Lord God shall give them light, and they shall reign forever.

COME, LORD JESUS

The Spirit and the Bride say, "Come!"

Rv 22:6-21

The angel said to me: "These words are trustworthy and true; the Lord, the God of prophetic spirits, has sent his angel to show his servants what must happen very soon."

"Remember, I am coming soon! Happy the man who heeds the prophetic message of this book!"

It is I, John, who heard and saw all these things, and when I heard and saw them I fell down to worship at the feet of the angel who showed them to me. But he said to me: "No, get up! I am merely a fellow servant with you and your brothers the prophets and those who heed the message of this book. Worship God alone!"

Then someone said to me: "Do not seal up the prophetic words of this book, for the appointed time is near! Let the wicked continue in their wicked ways, the depraved in their depravity! The virtuous must live on in their virtue and the holy ones in their holiness!"

"Remember, I am coming soon! I bring with me the reward that will be given to each man as his conduct deserves. I am the Alpha and the Omega, the First and the Last, the Beginning and the End. Happy are they who wash their robes so as to have free access to the tree of life and enter the city through its gates! Outside are the dogs and sorcerers, the fornicators and murderers, the idol-worshipers and all who love falsehood.

"It is I, Jesus, who have sent my angel to give you this testimony about the churches. I am the Root and Offspring of David, the Morning Star shining bright."

The Spirit and the Bride say, "Come!" Let him who hears answer, "Come!" Let him who is thirsty come forward; let all who desire it accept the gift of life-giving water.*

---

*See note on p. 232

The Holy Spirit in the Church

1. Prayers to the Holy Spirit

PRAYER OF POPE JOHN FOR THE SECOND VATICAN COUNCIL

Renew in our own days your miracles as of a second Pentecost

O divine Spirit, sent by the Father in the name of Jesus, give your aid and infallible guidance to your Church and pour out on the Ecumenical Council the fullness of your gifts.

O gentle Teacher and Consoler, enlighten the hearts of our prelates who, eagerly responding to the call of the Supreme Roman Pontiff, will gather here in solemn conclave.

May this Council produce abundant fruits; may the light and power of the gospel be more widely diffused in human society; may new vigor be imparted to the Catholic religion and its missionary function; may we all acquire a more profound knowledge of the Church's doctrine and a wholesome increase of Christian morality.

O gentle Guest of our souls, confirm our minds in truth and dispose our hearts to obedience, that the deliberations of the Council may find in us generous consent and prompt obedience.

We pray to you again for the lambs who are no longer part of the one fold of Jesus Christ, that they too, who still glory in the name of Christians, may at last be united under one shepherd.

Renew in our own days your miracles as of a second Pentecost; and grant that Holy Church, reunited in one prayer, more fervent than before, around Mary, the mother of Jesus, and under the leadership of Peter, may extend the kingdom of truth, justice, love and peace. Amen.

—*Journal of a Soul,* p. 391, copyright 1965, Geoffrey Chapman Ltd.

PRAYER OF THE COUNCIL FATHERS

O Holy Spirit. . . . Come abide with us

We are here before you, O Holy Spirit, conscious of our innumerable sins, but united in a special way in your holy name. Come and abide with us. Deign to penetrate our hearts.

Be the guide of our actions, indicate the path we should take, and show us what we must do so that, with your help, our work may be in all things pleasing to you.

May you be our only inspiration and the overseer of our intentions for you alone possess a glorious name together with the Father and the Son.

May you, who are infinite justice, never permit that we be disturbers of justice. Let not our ignorance induce us to evil, nor flattery sway us, nor moral and material interest corrupt us. But unite our hearts to you alone, and do it strongly, so that, with the gift of your grace, we may be one in you and may in nothing depart from the truth.

Thus, united in your name, may we in our every action follow the dictates of your mercy and justice,

so that today and always our judgments may not be
alien to you and in eternity we may obtain the unending
reward of our actions. Amen.

—*Documents of Vatican II*, p. xxii, copyright 1966,
The America Press.

INVOCATION OF THE HOLY SPIRIT

Come, Holy Spirit, fill the hearts of your faithful
    and kindle in them the fire of your divine love.

When you send forth your Spirit, they are created:
    And you renew the face of the earth.

O God,
on the first pentecost you instructed the hearts of those
    who believed in you
by the light of the Holy Spirit:
under the inspiration of the same Spirit,
give us a taste for what is right and true
and a continuing sense of his joy-bringing presence
    and power:
through Jesus Christ Our Lord.
Amen.

PRAYER TO THE HOLY SPIRIT

Heavenly King,
Consoler,
Spirit of truth,
present in all places and filling all things,
treasury of blessings and giver of life:
come and dwell in us,
cleanse us of every stain
and save our souls,
O gracious Lord.

Byzantine Liturgy

HYMN TO THE HOLY SPIRIT

Holy Spirit, font of light,
    focus of God's glory bright,
    shed on us a shining ray.
Father of the fatherless,
    giver of gifts limitless,
    come and touch our hearts today.
Source of strength and sure relief,
    comforter in time of grief,
    enter in and be our guest.
On our journey grant us aid,
    freshening breeze and cooling shade,
    in our labor inward rest.
Enter each aspiring heart,
    occupy its inmost part
    with your dazzling purity.
All that gives to man his worth,
    all that benefits the earth,
    you bring to maturity.
With your soft refreshing rains
    break our drought, remove our stains;
    bind up all our injuries.
Shake with rushing wind our will;
    melt with fire our icy chill;
    bring to light our perjuries.
As your promise we believe
    make us ready to receive
    gifts from your unbounded store.
Grant enabling energy,
    courage in adversity,
    joys that last for evermore.

PENTECOST SEQUENCE

Prose text of Hymn to the Holy Spirit

Come, Holy Spirit, and from heaven direct on man the rays of your light. Come, Father of the poor; come, giver of God's gifts; come, light of men's hearts.

Kindly Paraclete, in your gracious visits to man's soul you bring relief and consolation. If it is weary with toil, you bring it ease; in the heat of temptation, your grace cools it; if sorrowful, your words console it.

Light most blessed, shine on the hearts of your faithful—even into their darkest corners; for without your aid man can do nothing good, and everything is sinful.

Wash clean the sinful soul, rain down your grace on the parched soul and heal the injured soul. Soften the hard heart, cherish and warm the ice-cold heart, and give direction to the wayward.

Give your seven holy gifts to your faithful, for their trust is in you. Give them reward for their virtuous acts; give them a death that ensures salvation; give them unending bliss.

Amen. Alleluia.

LITANY TO THE SPIRIT

Come, Spirit of wisdom, and teach us to value the
    highest gift.
    Come, Holy Spirit.
Come, Spirit of understanding, and show us all things
    in the light of eternity.
    Come, Holy Spirit.
Come, Spirit of counsel, and guide us along the straight
    and narrow path to our heavenly home.
    Come, Holy Spirit.
Come, Spirit of might, and strengthen us against every
    evil spirit and interest which would separate us
    from you.
    Come, Holy Spirit.
Come, Spirit of knowledge, and teach us the shortness
    of life and the length of eternity.
    Come, Holy Spirit.
Come, Spirit of godliness, and stir up our minds and
    hearts to love and serve the Lord our God all our
    days.
    Come, Holy Spirit.
Come, Spirit of the fear of the Lord, and make us
    tremble with awe and reverence before your
    divine majesty.
    Come, Holy Spirit.

Traditional Hymn:

COME HOLY GHOST

Come, Holy Ghost, Creator blest,
And in our hearts take up thy rest.
Come with thy grace and heavenly aid
To fill the hearts which thou hast made
To fill the hearts which thou hast made.

Oh Comforter, to thee we cry,
Thou heavenly gift of God most high
Thou fount of life and fire of love
And sweet anointing from above
And sweet anointing from above.

Praise be to thee, Father and Son,
And Holy Spirit, with them one
And may the Son on us bestow
The gifts that from the Spirt flow
The gifts that from the Spirit flow.

2. Selections from Vatican II

THE HOLY SPIRIT IS THE SPIRIT OF LIFE

When the work that the Father gave the Son to do on earth (cf. Jn 17:4) was accomplished, the Holy Spirit was sent on the day of Pentecost in order that he might continually sanctify the Church, and thus, all those who believe would have access through Christ in one Spirit to the Father (cf. Eph 2:18). He is the Spirit of life, a fountain of water springing up to life eternal (cf. Jn 4:14; 7:38-39). To men, dead in sin, the Father gives life through him, until, in Christ, he brings to life their mortal bodies (cf. Rm 8:10-11). The Spirit dwells in the Church and in the hearts of the faithful as in a temple (cf. 1 Cor 3:16; 6:19). In them he prays on their behalf and bears witness to the fact that they are adopted sons (cf. Gal 4:6; Rm 8:15-16, 26). The Church, which he guides in the way of all truth (cf. Jn 16:13) and which he unifies in communion and in works of ministry, he both equips and directs with various hierarchical and charismatic gifts and adorns with his fruits (cf. Eph 4:11-12; 1 Cor 12:4; Gal 5:22). By the power of the Gospel he makes the Church keep the freshness of youth. Uninterruptedly he renews it and leads it to perfect union with its spouse. The Spirit and the bride both say to Jesus, the Lord, "Come!" (cf. Rv 22:17).

Thus, the Church is seen to be "a people made one with the unity of the Father, the Son and the Holy Spirit."—*Constitution on the Church,* 4

THE SPIRIT GIVES LIFE TO, UNIFIES AND MOVES THE WHOLE BODY

As all the members of the human body, though they are many, form one body, so also are the faithful in Christ (cf. 1 Cor. 12:12). So, in the building up of Christ's body a diversity of members and functions obtains. There is only one Spirit who, according to his own richness and the needs of the ministries, gives his different gifts for the welfare of the Church (cf. Cor 12:1-11). Among these gifts the grace of the apostles is preeminent. To their authority the Spirit himself subjected even those who were endowed with charisms (cf. 1 Cor 14). Giving the body unity through himself and through his power and inner joining of the members, this same Spirit produces and urges love among the believers. From all this it follows that if one member is honored, all the members rejoice together with it (cf. 1 Cor 12:26). . . .

In order that we might be unceasingly renewed in him (cf. Eph 4:23), he (Christ) has shared with us his Spirit who, being one and the same in the head and in the members, gives life to, unifies and moves the whole body in such a way that his work could be compared by the holy Fathers with the function that the principle of life, that is, the soul, fulfills in the human body.—*Constitution on the Church,* 7

THE HOLY SPIRIT DISTRIBUTES GIFTS
AMONG THE FAITHFUL OF EVERY RANK

It is not only through the sacraments and the ministries of the Church that the Holy Spirit sanctifies and leads the People of God and enriches it with virtues, but, "allotting his gifts to everyone according as he wills" (1 Cor 12:11), he distributes special graces among the faithful of every rank. By these gifts he makes them fit and ready to undertake the various tasks and duties which contribute toward the renewal and building up of the Church, according to the words of the apostle: "The manifestation of the Spirit is given to everyone for profit" (1 Cor 12:7). These charisms, whether they be the more outstanding or the more simple and widely diffused, are to be received with thanksgiving and consolation for they are especially suited to and useful for the needs of the Church. Extraordinary gifts are not to be rashly sought after, nor are the fruits of apostolic labor to be presumptuously expected from their use; but judgment as to their genuineness and proper use belongs to those who are leaders in the Church, and to whose special competence it belongs, not indeed to extinguish the Spirit, but to test all things and hold fast to that which is good (cf. 1 Thes 5:12; 19:21).
—*Constitution on the Church,* 12

ALL THEIR WORKS, IF CARRIED OUT
IN THE SPIRIT, BECOME "ACCEPTABLE"

The supreme and eternal priest, Christ Jesus, since he wills to continue his witness and service also through the laity, vivifies them in his Spirit and unceasingly urges them on to every good and perfect work.

For besides intimately linking them to his life and

his mission, he also gives them a share in his priestly function of offering spiritual worship for the glory of God and the salvation of men. For this reason the laity, dedicated to Christ and anointed by the Holy Spirit, are marvelously called and wonderfully prepared so that ever more abundant fruits of the Spirit may be produced in them. For all their works, prayers and apostolic endeavors, their ordinary married and family life, their daily occupations, their physical and mental relaxation, if carried out in the Spirit, and even the hardships of life, if patiently borne—all these become "spiritual sacrifices acceptable to God through Jesus Christ" (1 Pt 2:5).—*Constitution on the Church,* 34

THE HOLY SPIRIT IS THE
PRINCIPLE OF UNITY

After being lifted up on the cross and glorified, the Lord Jesus poured forth the Spirit whom he had promised, and through whom he has called and gathered together the people of the New Covenant, which is the Church, into a unity of faith, hope and charity, as the Apostle teaches us: "There is one body and one Spirit, just as you were called to the one hope of your calling; one Lord, one faith, one baptism" (Eph 4:4-5). For "all you who have been baptized into Christ have put on Christ . . . for you are all one in Christ Jesus" (Gal 3:27-28). It is the Holy Spirit dwelling in those who believe and pervading and ruling over the entire Church, who brings about the wonderful communion of the faithful and joins them together so intimately in Christ that he is the principle of the Church's unity. By distributing various kinds of spiritual gifts and ministries (cf. 1 Cor 12:4-11), he enriches the Church of Jesus Christ with different functions "in order to equip the saints for the work of service, so as to build up the body of Christ" (Eph 4:12).—*Decree on Ecumenism, 2*

THE HOLY SPIRIT WORKS FOR HOLINESS

The Holy Spirit works for the holiness of God's people through the sacraments and the service of ministry. To help them carry out their apostolate he also imparts to the faithful particular gifts which "he distributes among them just as he wishes" (1 Cor 12:13), in order that "each one may use whatever endowments he has received in the service of others," and thus become himself "a good steward of the manifold bounty of God" (1 Pt 4:10), for the building up of the whole body through love (cf. Eph 4:16). By possessing these charisms, even the ordinary ones, there arise for each of the faithful both the right and duty to use them in the Church and in the secular order for the well-being of mankind and growth of the Church. They are to be used in the freedom of the Holy Spirit who "breathes wherever he will" (Jn 3:8). They are to be used in mutual cooperation with all Christ's brothers, especially in cooperation with their pastors, whose duty it is to make judgment about the genuineness of these gifts and the disciplined use of them, not indeed "to extinguish the Spirit" (1 Thes 5:19), but "to test all things and to hold on to that which is good" (1 Thes 5:21).—*Decree on the Apostolate of the Laity, 3*

THE HOLY SPIRIT ASSISTS FAITH

"The obedience of faith" (Rm 13:26; cf. 1:5; 2 Cor 10:5-6) "is to be given to God who reveals, an obedience by which man commits his whole self freely to God, offering the full submission of intellect and will to God who reveals," and freely assenting to the truth revealed by him. To make this act of faith, the grace of God and the interior help of the Holy Spirit must precede and assist, moving the heart and turning it to God, opening the eyes of the mind and giving "joy and ease to everyone in assenting to the truth and believing it." To bring about an ever deeper understanding of revelation the same Holy Spirit constantly brings faith to completion by his gifts.—*Constitution on Divine Revelation,* 5

THE HOLY SPIRIT CONTINUES CHRIST'S WORK OF SALVATION

But everything the Lord said or did for man's salvation is to be proclaimed and disseminated to the ends of the earth, beginning from Jerusalem. Thus what was once accomplished for the salvation of all, should in time obtain its effects for everyone.

In order to achieve this, Christ sent the Holy Spirit from the Father, to continue the work of salvation in the hearts of men, and to animate the Church's growth. Certainly, the Holy Spirit was already operating in the world before Christ was glorified. But on Pentecost, the Spirit descended on the disciples to remain with them forever; the Church was publicly unveiled to the crowds; the spread of the Gospel to all peoples by preaching began; finally, on that day was foreshadowed the union of peoples in the catholicity of the faith, the

Church of the New Alliance. Because this Church speaks all languages, in its love, it understands and embraces all tongues, and thus overcomes the dispersion of Babel. On Pentecost the Acts of the Apostles began, just as Christ was conceived by the coming of the Holy Spirit on the Virgin Mary and impelled to begin his ministry by the same Spirit descending upon him while he prayed. Before freely laying down his life for the world, the Lord Jesus both prepared the ministry of the apostles and promised the sending of the Holy Spirit in such a way that both would be always and everywhere associated in bringing the work of salvation to completion. At all times, the Holy Spirit unifies the whole Church "in union and in service and endows it with different hierarchical and charismatic gifts," animating ecclesiastical institutions almost like a soul and instilling in the hearts of the faithful the same spirit of mission which moved Christ. Sometimes the Spirit also anticipated the work of the apostles just as he unceasingly accompanies and directs it in various ways.—*Decree on the Missionary Activity of the Church,* 3.4

THE PEOPLE OF GOD
IS LED BY THE LORD'S SPIRIT . . .
(TO) THE DIVINE PLAN

The People of God believes that it is led by the Lord's Spirit, who fills the earth. Motivated by this faith, it labors to decipher authentic signs of God's presence and purpose in the happenings, needs and desires in which this People has a part along with other men of our age. For faith throws a new light on everything, manifests God's design for man's total vocation, and thus directs the mind to solutions which are fully human. . . .

The intellectual nature of the human person is perfected by wisdom and needs to be, for wisdom gently attracts the mind of man to a quest and a love for what is true and good. Steeped in wisdom, man passes through visible realities to those which are unseen.

Our era needs such wisdom more than bygone ages if the discoveries made by man are to be further humanized. For the future of the world stands in peril unless wiser men are forthcoming. . . .

It is, finally, through the gift of the Holy Spirit that man comes by faith to the contemplation and appreciation of the divine plan.—*Constitution on the Church in the Modern World,* 11, 15

THE HOLY SPIRIT RENEWS THE WHOLE MAN

The Christian man, conformed to the likeness of that
Son who is the firstborn of many brothers, received "the
firstfruits of the Spirit" (Rm 8:23) by which he becomes
capable of discharging the new law of love. Through this
Spirit, who is "the pledge of our inheritance" (Eph 1:14),
the whole man is renewed from within, even to the
achievement of "the redemption of the body" (Rm
8:23): "If the Spirit of him who raised Jesus from the
dead dwells in you, then he who raised Jesus Christ
from the dead will also bring to life your mortal bodies
because of his Spirit who dwells in you" (Rm 8:11).
Pressing upon the Christian, to be sure, are the need
and the duty to battle against evil through manifold
tribulations and even to suffer death. But, linked with
the paschal mystery and patterned on the dying Christ,
he will hasten forward to resurrection in the strength
which comes from hope.

All this holds true not only for Christians, but for
all men of good will in whose hearts grace works in an
unseen way. For, since Christ died for all men, and
since the ultimate vocation of man is in fact one, and
divine, we ought to believe that the Holy Spirit in a
manner known only to God offers to every man the
possibility of being associated with the paschal mystery.

Such is the mystery of man, and it is a great one,
as seen in believers in the light of Christian revelation.
Through Christ and in Christ, the riddles of sorrow and
death grow meaningful. Apart from his Gospel, they
overwhelm us. Christ has risen, destroying death by
his death; he has lavished life upon us so that, as sons in
the Son, we can cry out in the Spirit: *Abba,* Father!—
Constitution on the Church in the Modern World, 22

CHRIST IS NOW AT WORK
IN THE HEARTS OF MEN
THROUGH THE ENERGY OF HIS SPIRIT

To those, therefore, who believe in divine love, he gives
assurance that the way of love lies open to men and
that the effort to establish a universal brotherhood is not
a hopeless one. He cautions them at the same time
that this charity is not something to be reserved for
important matters, but must be pursued chiefly in the
ordinary circumstances of life. Undergoing death itself
for all of us sinners, he taught us by example that we too
must shoulder that cross which the world and the flesh
inflict upon those who search after peace and justice.
Appointed Lord by his resurrection and given plenary
power in heaven and on earth, Christ is now at work in
the hearts of men through the energy of the Holy Spirit,
arousing not only a desire for the age to come, but by
that very fact animating, purifying and strengthening
those noble longings too by which the human family
makes its life more human and strives to render the whole
earth submissive to this goal.

Now, the gifts of the Spirit are diverse: while he
calls some to give clear witness to the desire for a
heavenly home and to keep that desire green among
the human family, he summons others to dedicate themselves to the earthly service of men and to make ready
the material of the celestial realm by this ministry of
theirs. Yet he frees all of them so that by putting aside
love of self and bringing all earthly resources into the
service of human life they can devote themselves to that
future when humanity itself will become an offering
accepted by God.—*Constitution on the Church in the
Modern World,* 38

3. Two excerpts from Paul VI

**THE HOLY SPIRIT AND THE
LIFE OF THE CHURCH**

On what does the Church live? The question is addressed
to that which is the eternal principle of its life; the
original principle which distinguishes the Church from
every other society; an indispensable principle, just as
breathing is for man's physical life; a divine principle
which makes a son of earth a son of heaven and confers
on the Church its mystical personality: the Holy Spirit.
The Church lives on the Holy Spirit. The Church was
truly born, you could say, on the day of Pentecost.
The Church's first need is always to live Pentecost. . . .

It is in the Holy Spirit that the twofold union is
perfected—that of the Church with Christ and with
God, and that of the Church with all its members, the
faithful. It is the Holy Spirit who gives life to the whole
body of the Church and to its individual members by
means of that intimate action which we call grace. . . .

If the Church lives on the illuminating and sanctifying
inspiration of the Holy Spirit, then the Church has a
need of the Holy Spirit: a basic need, an existential need,
a need that cannot be satisfied with illusions, with
substitutes . . . a universal need, a permanent need. . . .

At this point, someone might raise the objection:

But doesn't the Church already possess the Holy Spirit? Isn't this need already satisfied? Yes, of course, the Church already and forever possesses the Holy Spirit. But first of all, his action admits of various degrees and circumstances, so that our action is needed too, if the activity of the Holy Spirit is to be free and full; and secondly, the Holy Spirit's presence in individual souls can diminish or be missing entirely. This is why the word of God is preached and the sacraments of grace are distributed; this is why people pray and why each individual tries to merit the great "gift of God," the Holy Spirit, for himself and for the whole Church.

For this reason, if we really love the Church, the main thing we must do is to foster in it an outpouring of the divine Paraclete, the Holy Spirit. And if we accept the ecclesiology of the Council, which lays so much stress on the action of the Holy Spirit in the Church . . . then we should be glad to accept its guideline for fostering the Church's vitality and renewal, and for orientating our own personal Christian lives along these lines.

Where does this guideline lead us? Toward the Holy Spirit. . . . The Spirit who makes us Christians and raises us to supernatural life, is the true and profound principle of our interior life and of our external apostolic activity. . . .

—Paul VI, General Audience, October 12, 1966
(Tr. from *The Pope Speaks* (Washington, D.C.): 12, 1967, pp. 79-81)

THE BREATH OF THE HOLY SPIRIT

We have asked ourselves on several occasions what are the greatest needs of the Church. . . .

(The Church needs): the Spirit, the Holy Spirit, the animator and sanctifier . . . her divine breath, . . . her unifying principle, her inner source of light and strength, her support and consoler, her source of charisms and songs, her peace and her joy. . . .

The Church needs her perennial Pentecost; she needs fire in the heart, words on the lips, prophecy in the glance. The Church needs to be the temple of the Holy Spirit. . . . She needs to feel within her, in the silent emptiness of us modern men, all turned outwards because of the spell of exterior life, charming, fascinating, corrupting with delusions of false happiness, to feel rising from the depths of her inmost personality . . . the praying voice of the Spirit, who, as St. Paul teaches us, takes our place and prays in us and for us "with sighs too deep for words," and who interprets the words that we by ourselves would not be able to address to God. . . .

Living men, you young people, and you consecrated souls, you brothers in the priesthood, are you listening to us? This is what the Church needs. She needs the Holy Spirit. The Holy Spirit in us, in each of us, and in all of us together, in us who are the Church. . . .

So let all of you ever say to him, "Come!"

—Paul VI, General Audience, November 29, 1972
(Tr. from *L'Osservatore Romano,* December 7, 1972)

CONCORDANCE - INDEX

THE PENTATEUCH

THE HISTORICAL BOOKS

THE WISDOM BOOKS

THE PROPHETS

ISAIAH

260

THE GOSPELS

MATTHEW

MARK

LUKE

THE ACTS OF THE APOSTLES

THE EPISTLES OF PAUL

1 CORINTHIANS

267

2 CORINTHIANS

GALATIANS

THESSALONIANS

TIMOTHY AND TITUS

THE OTHER EPISTLES AND REVELATION

HEBREWS

JAMES AND PETER